Now We Are
Thirtysomething

Charles Jennings is a writer and journalist whose work has appeared in *The Sunday Times, Tatler, The Telegraph, Cosmopolitan* and *GQ*. He is the author of *The Confidence Trick*. He is also a dramatist writing for radio and television, including Thames TV's hugely successful series 'Capital City'. He is married with two children and lives in London.

Now We Are Thirtysomething

Charles Jennings

JOHN MURRAY

© Charles Jennings 1991

First published in 1991
by John Murray (Publishers) Ltd
50 Albemarle Street, London W1X 4BD

The right of Charles Jennings to be identified as
the author of this work has been asserted by him
in accordance with the Copyright, Designs and Patents Act, 1988.

British Library Cataloguing in Publication Data
Jennings, Charles
    Now we are thirtysomething.
    I. Title
    828.91409

    ISBN 0-7195-4958-2

Designed by Gaye Allen
Typeset by Rowland Phototypesetting Ltd,
Bury St Edmunds, Suffolk
Printed and bound in Great Britain by
Butler and Tanner Ltd, Frome and London

To Dante, who said it all, really:

Nel mezzo del cammin di nostra vita
mi ritrovai per una selva oscura
che la diritta via era smarrita.

Acknowledgements

Today newspaper, for its unfailing obsession with young-middle-aged people; *She* magazine, for its unhealthy interest in sexual matters; Waitrose, for the coffee; The Dame Lettice Prosser School of Touch-Typing; The London Borough of Richmond Upon Thames, for the use of its libraries; Caroline Knox, for editing; Sam Kydd and Thorley Walters, for greatness; Creamola ('The Very Good Pudding'), for inspiration; *Exchange & Mart*, for style hints; Andrew, Sassy, Katherine, John, Caroline, Derek, Emma, Clare, Peta, Chris, Ali, Geraldine, Jon, Ivan, Paul, Stella, Magnus, Alistair, Timothy and Susie (the wife) for suggestions, examples, obstructions and critique.

The author and publishers would like to credit the following for the use of their advertisements in the book: The Badedas Company, Belling & Co. Ltd., Butlins Ltd., Hornby Hobbies Ltd., KLM, Kodak Ltd., Lever Bros. Ltd., Nestlé Co. Ltd., Ratners Group plc., Rover Cars, United Distillers, Vauxhall Motors Ltd.

Acknowledgement is due to the following for kindly giving permission to reproduce copyright material: *The Sunday Times*, Methuen London for extracts from *Mothers* by Bretecher, *Pure Posy* by Posy Simmonds, *File Under Biff* by Chris Garratt & Mick Kidd and Monitor Syndication for the photograph of Victoria Wood.

Every effort has been made to trace copyright holders. In some cases this has proved impossible. The author and publishers would be pleased to hear from any copyright holder not acknowledged.

Cartoons on pages 1, 13, 22, 45, 57, 61, 71, 89, 99, 106, 116 © David Austin. Cartoons on pages 25, 51, 83 © Sue Heap

Contents

We Are . . .

. . . Ten years of thirtyish people, now coming onstream.

In fact, our two great historical ages are the 1950s and the 1970s. The Fifties lasted well into the Sixties, thanks to our parents. They called the shots while we were still tiny, and *they* didn't spring into crushed velvet bell-bottoms in 1966, just because it was a happening thing to do. They, and the schools we went to, helped preserve a brown Fifties environment all through our early years. For us, the Sixties were never more than a distant rumour overheard on Radio Caroline.

But the Seventies were *ours*. That low, dishonest decade was when we broke free of our parents, banished the Fifties, discovered that we'd missed the Sixties, and tried to make the best of it with an orgy of revolting clothes, tasteless music and formless *anomie*.

But now, twenty years on, we have the money. We are getting the power. We're the doers, the opinion-makers. (You want TV? Victoria Wood, Jeremy Paxman. You want stage? Emma Thompson, Daniel Day Lewis. You want music? Nigel Kennedy. You want politics? Tony Blair. You want journos? Ian Hislop, Julie Burchill, Linda Kelsey. And on it goes.)

I FEEL I'M <u>SOMEBODY</u> AT LAST, BUT I'M NOT SURE WHO.

Our activities fill the newspapers and magazines – siring more children; making, or failing to make, ends meet; grappling with the intricacies of our lives as workers, parents, divorcees. Advertisers yearn for us. We see ourselves everywhere, smirking on billboards, lounging on the pages of colour magazines, parading around in TV commercials. No ad is complete without a small, clean child in it, coddled by a relaxed 27-year-old model pretending to be a 32-year-old.

Yes: we are the . . . the . . . What exactly *are* we?

We are, in a word, busy. Ridiculously busy. We've gone from a more-or-less carefree kind of life – the life of our twenties, in which the car, the flat and the girlfriend/boyfriend were about the only real constituents – to a world in which *everyone* wants a piece of our time, in which we have to make decisions (fundamental, trivial, pregnant with import) every three minutes.

Something has happened to our shops. With the general collapse of time, and the mad rush to Get Things Done, practices like loitering in nice little delicatessens and antique shops and little designer clothing establishments and framed print emporia, have gone west.

This is where we shop, now:

Marks & Spencer
W. H. Smith
Mothercare
Sainsbury's
Dixons
Our Price Records
Waterstone's
Majestic Wines
Oddbins
Waitrose
Rymans
Dolcis
Comet
C&A
John Lewis
Safeway

That's it. Chainstores. We now live our lives by the computer stock charts of vast plcs.

We have kids. And if we don't have kids we are either trying to have them or wondering why we're not having them (maybe we haven't settled down like all our friends: is something *wrong* with us?).

And kids mean money – not money like throw-it-away 1986 money, but chronic money: money which goes slice by slice into the mortgage, the pension plan, the life insurance, the repairs to the house (yes, it's goodbye rank, noisy little flat and hallo four bedrooms somewhere quieter now that the family's started), school fee plans, nappies, baby clothes, holidays in DIY villas in southern France, and the bigger car to get you, the kids, and their impedimenta to the DIY villa.

We have accountants, and we have men who smell of industrial aftershave who call themselves our financial advisers. We have made our wills. We have joined a health care programme. We are putting on weight. We have either (a) at last got somewhere in our jobs and like it (but we have to work damn hard), or (b) are seriously thinking about making a change.

We have parents who seem to have lurched abruptly into grand-parenthood, or who are nagging us to *make* them grandparents. We are getting divorced, after the first flush of twenties marriages.

3

We spend years at home, living, eating, decorating, cleaning up, drinking, watching TV and listening to music. Our homes and our relaxations have become the building-blocks of our lives. Sometimes we take holidays, full of meaning and anticipation. We have diaries crammed with great events and absolute futilities.

That's the thing about the thirties: there's so much *of* them.

Some Thirtyish Heroes

Victoria Wood
Tony Blair
Adrian Edmondson
Jeremy Paxman
Julie Burchill
Emma Thompson
Nigel Mansell
Lenny Henry
Nigel Kennedy
Ian Hislop
Linda Kelsey

Please insert your comments in the space provided:

....

....

A day in the life

It was a morning much like any other for Claire and Steven Whitelock . . .

7·15 Both sleep through *Today* on the radio. Bizarre dreams involving US Secretary of State, Minister for Ag. & Fish, woman involved in dispute with her council about pest control . . .

7·34 Claire springs into bathroom with cry of rage (the train *goes* at 8.21). Steven nicks himself with a safety razor that can't nick you.

7·59 No Shreddies.

8·21 No train. Claire smoulders on platform, aware of glaring discrepancy between left earring and right earring.

8·34 Steven manages to turn car right at end of road after seven-minute wait for break in the traffic. Please God, not Libby Purves on the radio. Please God, let me get to the office before nine o'clock.

8·46 Train arrives. Delayed due to staff shortages. Claire now conscious of rogue hairstyle, lopsidedly dangling over left eye.

9·01 Libby Purves on radio. Two miles still to go.

9·16 Claire sprints into work. This observation nags away at her: why is everything covered in clocks these days? There is a clock on the cooker; another on the video; another on the dashboard of the car; another built in to the pocket-calculator; yet another on the end of the pen she uses; another on the device that switches the boiler on and off; yet another on the outside of the tall building Steven passes in his car on the flyover. Why do we need to be reminded about the eradication of time all the time?

So far, the morning has gone in a blur. Now it speeds up to an eyeblink. It's ten o'clock. Then it's half past eleven. What *happened*? Isn't there ever a time when time slows down? When we're bored? When we're uncomfortable? When we're travelling? When we're in love? When we're waiting to be paid? Why did time move into fifth gear on her thirtieth birthday?

9·21 This is when time drops into bottom gear. When you're stuck in traffic with Libby Purves on radio. Steven hunts for tape to play. Finds only *Music Of The Pyrenees* from last holiday, unplayed.

11·15 Claire paddles away at buttons on telephone, scours desk for material to take to meeting (3.00 p.m., the worst) gets hung up fielding call from incandescent client wanting to know why contract has been mis-drafted for third time in succession . . .

9·33 Steven is in an alternative time zone now. Libby Purves shows no sign of ending. Traffic no sign of starting. What is time when you're in a company hatchback surrounded by sweating execs in their hatchbacks, furiously scanning the radio for something other than Libby Purves? Makes note: get car 'phone. Bloke supposed to come in for new business pitch will have got there by now. Not in same jam, by any chance?

12·46 Time (concludes Claire, on her way to the sarnie bar for a beef and mayo special) is both plastic and inexorable. FUCK! She's forgotten the copies for the directors!

9·48 Steven gets a local radio station on FM. Didn't even know local radio station existed. Who the hell listens to it? People in traffic jams? Bloke in business pitch probably about to leave. Why bother? Why not turn round, go home, phone in and say, working from home today? Why not? Because gap suddenly opens in traffic and . . .

12·59 No time to eat, no time to . . .

10·00 Get in to work! Bloke due for business pitch hasn't even *arrived* !!

13·16 Steven checks watch: It's 1.16! Three hours at work already . . .

14·48 Meeting changed to room on fourth floor from room on seventh floor. Does everyone know this? Numbers on Claire's watch resemble numbers of her bank account, going wrong way . . . 14.48 up to 15.00 up to 15.01 . . .

15·04   Steven totters to caff round corner with Brian from Personnel. Just a quick cup of coffee and a bun. *Quick.*

15·16   Meeting starts in room on fourth floor. Takes ten minutes forty-two seconds just for everyone to agree that they're all there. Nearly half-past three. Which is almost four o'clock.

15·54   Almost four o'clock! *Fuck!* Got to call opposite number in Coventry office about outstanding claim . . .

16·22   Meeting time not like any other sort of time. Manages to be endless, dreary, absurdly protracted, pointless, blank, and yet, simultaneously, to pass quickly. Claire tries not to fall asleep. Head of Corporate Relations twats on in gathering dusk. Claire looks at watch. Fifteen minutes have sped by. How? Corporate Relations bore speaking at normal speed. How come time speeds up and slows down all at once?

17·47   Steven looks up from call to opposite number in Coventry. *That's* how long it took? Just to say that claim had been processed at his end, had all relevant documentation, etc. Rest of time must have gone on fruitless speculations as to why Coventry end without similar paperwork, could it be in

8

post room, could it be mistake of Coventry end's secretary, did Coventry end actually *have it on desk but hadn't looked*? Does Steven stay to wrap up report he planned to wrap up before lunch or leave it till next day? Looks out of window. Traffic. Take hour and a quarter to get home. Might as well stay, wrap up report . . .

18·23 Claire falls through front door of house. Heads for fridge. No cold mineral water. Drinks it warm. Time begins to slow down.

19·31 Steven falls through front door of house. Heads for fridge. Where beer secreted last night? Remembers to kiss Claire.

20·16 Claire, Steven and TV . . . Claire listlessly consults diary. Remember following: dinner at Watsons' house, Friday. Wedding of The Pervert to Queen Victoria, Saturday. Drink on Sunday at – *where wedding present?* Present completely unbought! But *when* to buy the bugger?

21·43 Steven lies unconscious in bath. Claire debates what to buy Pervert and Queen Victoria. Decides on silver picture frame. Tells unconscious Steven that he'll have to buy it, he's nearest to weathered antique shop with charming tat in window. Is that understood? Steven dreams of driving his car swiftly and effortlessly over thrilling lanes and highways . . . not realizing how Saturday will come, no present bought for Pervert and Queen, will have to leap into car, 11.08 Saturday morning, claw through Saturday traffic to near place of work, double-park car, run into weathered antique shop, snatch slightly unsuitable rococo frame from shelf, pay with desperate ACCESS he was trying to cut down on, emerge, tear ticket from windscreen, drive recklessly home, fling frame at Claire, discover best shirt in fact dirty and get to wedding with three minutes to spare . . .

22·46 Claire drifts into sleep . . . Steven reads important novel by Julian Barnes.

22·47 Steven falls asleep. Time collapses. Until voice of Brian Redhead erupts into nightmare about taking exam in Ancient Greek . . .

The Seventies

Strange, inadmissible nostalgia for the Seventies . . . after all, they were the years in which we were young. They were the years in which we began to grow up; in which we started to discover who it was we thought we'd like to be; in which our earliest (and therefore longest-lasting) preferences in love, music, pleasure were formed.

The Seventies – whether from '69 to '76 or from '76 to '80 (the great Punk divide) – were our decade. They shaped us. They're ours.

People have written fondly about the Fifties:

And they've written fondly about the Sixties:

‘ Of all the provincial cities we visited regularly it was Manchester which continued to supply forbidden stories on a lavish scale. It was here for example that Ian and Mick discovered the Caterers' Club, and full of enthusiasm took me there on grey afternoon after the pubs shut. It was a small room with a bar, originally a shop but with the window boarded up. It was lit by naked bulbs, the floor was bare boards, and on the wall was a hand-made poster which said. "Try our cocktail, 1s. 6d." . . . The clientele were low-grade villains of a Dickensian aspect and the oldest whores in the world . . . ’

GEORGE MELLY, *Owning-Up*

‘ The first time I came out of my shell was when I saw The Who at the Marquee. I'd never seen anything like it. I couldn't imagine that people could do such things. I went straight out and broke a window, I was that impressed . . . ’

‘ . . . UFO was exotic, but it wasn't nearly as memorable for me as Middle Earth. Middle Earth took your breath away. It was the whole situation of it, in the middle of Covent Garden when it *was* Covent Garden. You'd go through these desolate, wet streets into this basement in King Street, just near the Opera House. Into this great space filled with music and incense and drugs, this great huge warehouse with pineapples and bananas. Light-shows going. You'd go out on this wonderful surge. You'd rendezvous with people at midnight at Covent Garden station. We had our own little universe, you'd walk in, everyone knew you, you'd say "Hi" to Jeff . . . ’

From *Days In The Life – Voices From The English Underground*, compiled by Jonathan Green.

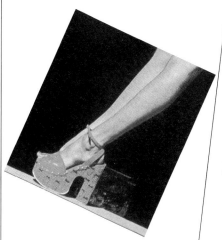

Much of what we feel, what we most remember from those times, is a sense of having missed the party. The great public figures – the Kennedys, Dr Martin Luther King, The Beatles – had gone. Ideals, the promised revolutions of '68, had lapsed into churlishness. The larger world gave the impression of being locked in an eternal, stuffy, irritable embrace of opposites: Americans with Russians; governments with trade unions; the young with the middle-aged. We'd arrived too late to enjoy whatever it was that the Sixties had; and we were left the warm dregs to mull over.

Consider this litany:

- Skinheads
- Elton John LPs
- Slade
- The Austin Maxi
- Sideburns
- No. 6's
- Getting the clap
- Flares that collected the dirt

- Vic Feather
- The EEC referendum
- The Raymond Froggatt Band
- Ker-Nockers
- The Wombles
- *Long Haired Lover From Liverpool*, by Little Jimmy Osmond

Shocking, isn't it? Almost nothing that endures. Except, of course, that it does endure, in our memories and in the way we see the world now. And what obscure joy we get from recalling the Seventies in the company of another Seventies survivor. What do we feel when we describe to each other our LP collections of sixteen years ago, when we linger on the morose pleasures of vodka and lime, inept discos, French kissing, Watney's Party-Seven beer, cheesecloth shirts, Budgie jackets, very long floral skirts, knee-length boots with zips in the side, army greatcoats, Mateus Rosé, and tank tops . . . Our generation is sitting on a mountain of uncelebrated memories.

What values do we bring with us? We grew up in a world of chainstore high fashion, middle-of-the-road revolution, cover-version original pop music. So what does that make us today? Do we now feel a compulsion to *believe* things again? Do we want a friendly ideology to call our own? (Nothing too demonstrative, because we all remember what happened to the Maoists, Trotskyites, Stalinists and Diggers of the '70s). Are we looking for sincerity, value for money, and good design features?

THE SEVENTIES: A GUIDE

POLITICS • CURRENT AFFAIRS • ECONOMICS • WARS • ETC.

I'VE MOVED FROM THE APOLITICAL LEFT TO THE APOLITICAL RIGHT

1970

The age of majority is reduced from 21 to 18 in Britain.

1971

Decimal currency is introduced. Two things. Who remembers the public-service training films they used to show on TV, round about news time, with words and music by – The Scaffold? – introducing us to the prospect of the 2p and the 5p and so on? *And* – who was Lord Fiske of the Decimal Currency Board (ah, glorious corporatist Labour party designation, The Decimal Currency Board) and why did he say that 'All was going well' when nobody except the very young or very bright could understand a thing?

1972

Britain signs the treaty which will bring it into the EEC the following year. Other signatories: Ireland, Denmark and Norway.

More important, there was a miners' strike which resulted in the three-day week, comprehensive power cuts and enormous disruption. Remember trying to study for your O's and A's by candlelight? Crouched over the table at home endeavouring to scarf up all those little facts they required of you in those days (what *is* Bauxite? when should you employ *j'eusse, tu eusses, il eusse*? what are the consequences of heating copper in a stream of chlorine gas?) and praying that the fuckers would leave the lights on until you'd done *just this bit*? Or even leave them on long enough for you to watch TV?

If you were working, though, the thing reversed itself: and you longed for the office lights to blink out, and the old Smith-Corona to die under your fingertips . . .

1973

The Yom Kippur War left Britain with an oil shortage: the prospect of petrol coupons, rationing, vast, ill-tempered queues of motorists (lines of Maxis, Marinas, Triumphs,

Look what's included with Viva

One of the joys of owning a '73 Viva is that the most important 'extras' are included in the basic price. From the 1256 cc 2-door de Luxe Viva (price £944) upwards, all have heated rear window, power-assisted front discs, wall-to-wall carpet, fitted front seat belts, alternator, and a complete,

factory-applied underbody seal.

Viva gives you the basic things too. A lively engine. A comfortable ride. Room for four people to travel in comfort and style.

Test-drive a Viva soon – see how much extra it brings to family motoring.

Sunbeams, Jensens and other vanished motoring tat . . .) trailing out of shabby petrol stations. The miners were agitating *again*. The TV went off at 10.30. Why were the '70s spent in a semi-permanent state of wartime privation? No sooner had you got used to being able to have the lights on whenever you wanted, than you (or Dad) had to trail down to the BP station with a jerry-can in your hand and beg for half a gallon of four-star. It made you wonder quite what the point of prosperity was, since you could never wholly enjoy it.

1974

Nixon resigns; meanwhile, thousands of miles away, 'Lucky' Lucan, the toff with the moronic rakehell stare and the Groucho Marx moustache, goes missing, leaving a dead nanny behind . . .

1975

Vietnam War ends. Thatcher is voted in as Tory leader. EEC referendum shabbily confirms that 67 per cent of us say Yes. First time you got to vote? And was it worth it? At last, you exercise the franchise, and with trembling hand inscribe your X on the slip of paper.

1976

Resignation: Wilson evaporates in March. Almost immediately, a heatwave descends on the rest of Britain. Denis Howell is created the Minister for Drought, and the temperature in London reaches 35°C (95°F). We're used to it now, of course, but at the time it seemed rather exciting. And it helped to maintain that crazy '70s wartime austerity, by forcing millions of us to flush the lavatory with our bathwater, boil potatoes in the fish pond and wait in yet more queues, this time for standpipe water. The drought was officially broken on 31 August, by which time much of the country was incinerated and our clothes (especially those interesting snug-fit polyester shirts) were destroyed with sweat.

1977

Nothing happens.

1978

After a brief lapse, Fate booked us in for more hardship. The bakers went on strike. The bakers! We didn't even realize that they organized their labour collectively, until Panic Buying (a great '70s pastime, Panic Buying – of salt, sugar and so on) set in at the beginning of November. So now we had electricity, petrol and water, and ineffable home-made bread which had the consistency of baked plaster.

1979

The rest is history . . . Winter of Discontent boxes Callaghan in, people of Britain get so sick of futile *Nostalgie de la Blitz* privations that they vote in Thatcher, 4 May. History turns the page, and just as the Seventies really begin in 1969, so the Eighties really start in 1979. (No end to the privations, though. They just keep on going.)

• FILMS •

We watch the films of the 1970s almost non-stop on TV. And they're especially evocative, not just because they're detailed period pieces (just *look* at those sideburns) but because they so often recall the circumstances in which we first watched them. Think about it: why did we go to the cinema, in those days? It was still new, exciting, a treat. X-certificate films were within our grasp. We went to town with our rank, spotty friends, looking for sleaze. *We took our boyfriends and our girlfriends.* A whole mass of events and emotions accompanied each trip to the cinema.

And when we watch these films again, fifteen years later, how often do we find ourselves drawn back to the world in which we first saw them? *Cabaret* or *Annie Hall*: when we watch a re-run on the box, we can be overwhelmed by the most unexpected nostalgia.

Big Powerful Slightly Dull Films:

THE DEER HUNTER (1978)

THE GODFATHER (1971)

APOCALYPSE NOW (1979)

Art Movies:

CABARET (1972)

PICNIC AT HANGING ROCK (1975)

SITTING DUCKS (1978)

THE MARRIAGE OF MARIA BRAUN (1978)

THE TREE OF WOODEN CLOGS (1978)

DEATH IN VENICE (1971)

DON'T LOOK NOW (1973)

CARNAL KNOWLEDGE (1971)

ONE FLEW OVER THE CUCKOO'S NEST (1975)

Smut:

EMMANUELLE (1974)

LAST TANGO IN PARIS (1972)

IMMORAL TALES (1974)

AI NO CORRIDA (1976)

Humour:

ANNIE HALL (1977)

LA CAGE AUX FOLLES (1978)

MONTY PYTHON'S LIFE OF BRIAN (1979)

THE RETURN OF THE PINK PANTHER (1974)

PLAY IT AGAIN, SAM (1972)

Action Movies/Popular Junk:

BUTCH CASSIDY AND THE SUNDANCE KID (1969)

STAR WARS (1977)

THE TOWERING INFERNO (1974)

THE FRENCH CONNECTION (1971)

ROCKY II (1979)

JAWS (1975)

GREASE (1978)

•CULTURE •SPORT • TELEVISION • HOT PANTS •

An assortment of turning-points:

1 Your first sight of Reg Varney in *On The Buses*.
2 Evonne Goolagong wins the Wimbledon Women's Singles Final, July 1971. The moment when a million pubescent boys took an unwonted interest in the game.
3 Streaking becomes popular.
4 *The Daily Sketch* goes out of business, May 1971.
5 You read *The Lord Of The Rings*, and J. R. R. Tolkien dies in September 1973. You invest in a Bilbo Baggins poster for your bedroom wall. You are told that this is the book in which Tolkien never uses the word 'the'.
6 Carl André places his bricks in the Tate Gallery (1976) and you realize

17

abruptly that you are a passionate aesthete, welcoming André's challenge to preconceptions about art, space, detail. You argue furiously and pointlessly with your parents and any other dopes who *just can't see what he's doing*.

7 Reginald Bosanquet resigns from ITN, November 1979.

8 Bobby Fischer beats Boris Spassky and becomes the first US chess champion: posing the question, Where is Reykjavik?

9 Anthony Powell finishes his twelve-part novel sequence *A Dance To The Music of Time* (1975). Inspired to prove your aesthetic credentials (pre-Carl André), you vow to read the whole lot. Do you read the whole lot, or read the first one and the last one and guess the rest? Do you start on *A Question of Upbringing* and throw it away after twelve pages (*my God this book's abysmally badly written and boring*)? Do you ever find out why 'smart' people pronounce the author's surname as if it were spelt *Pole*?

10 Bill Grundy has trouble with The Sex Pistols on TV. You miss the encounter, but realize abruptly that you are a Blank Generation Kid going Nowhere on a Fast Track to Nothingness, and start spitting obscenely in deserted playgrounds.

11 Last episode of *Dixon of Dock Green*. Part of your early childhood dies with it.

12 You see at least one of the following musicals: *Hair, Jesus Christ Superstar, Godspell, Joseph*

And The Amazing Technicolour Dreamcoat, The Rocky Horror Show. You attempt to debauch your girlfriend as a consequence of nos 1 and 5. As a consequence of nos 2, 3, 4, she gives you a T-shirt with *Have You Met Jesus To-Day?* printed on the front.

• MUSIC •

What we think of as the music we used to listen to, isn't necessarily the music that was played to us. A familiar disjunction: while we hold on to personal musical favourites dating back over twenty-five years because we still enjoy listening to them, the music which brings on the fiercest nostalgia is often a terrible, loathsome noise with which we think we have nothing in common. *Cheap music.*

For every five hours we spent hugger-mugger over *The Dark Side of the Moon*, we spent ten minutes listening to *Kung Fu Fighting* by Carl Douglas. For every evening wasted in the contemplation of *Tubular Bells*, we spent no more than the time it takes to finish a vodka-and-lime soaking up *Sugar Baby Love* by the Rubettes. But the appalling Carl Douglas and Rubettes are just as potent salvagers of memory as Mike Oldfield and the Pink Floyd, because theirs was the music of harrowing, lust-ridden parties and halitotic discos; theirs was the music which made up the soundtrack of the most exciting moments of our lives.

This disjunction does not trouble our thirty-something lives, partly because we no longer enjoy the same moments of sexual and personal discovery, and partly because those lives are generally so ordered nowadays that *all* our tastes are admissible. A sign of our having grown up is not just that we wouldn't listen to a Top Twenty single even if by any chance we could, but that we organize life so that we will never have to listen, by chance, to a Top Twenty single. Our mature tastes forbid the chance of cheap music.

But these awful songs *were* the soundtracks of our lives: *Clair*, by Gilbert O'Sullivan; *Bang Bang* by B. A. Robertson; *Chirpy Chirpy Cheep*

Cheep, by Middle of the Road; *Knowing Me Knowing You*, by AВBA; *Gonna Make You A Star*, by David Essex; *I Wanna Dance Wit Choo*, by Disco Tex and the Sex-o-lettes.

Once again we lapse into passive resentment of the children of the Sixties, who can now revisit their abandoned younger selves *and* listen to wonderful pop songs at the same time. They lived their lives to The Beatles, Smokey Robinson, The Beach Boys, The Kinks. The soundtrack of *The Big Chill* really is the soundtrack to their lives. What they miss, however, is a certain corrupt pleasure which only we can enjoy: the pleasure of memory made sweeter by the fact that such noxious art recalls it. 'These exercises offer the completest abandon, the most monstrous intemperance, the most total abasement . . .'

Greatest Hits of the Seventies

(As published in *Record Mirror*)

1970

Best-selling single – *The Wonder of You*, Elvis Presley. Still alive, and ready to go on until August 1977.
Best-selling album – *Bridge Over Troubled Water*, Simon & Garfunkel. Timeless tunes & thinning hair.

1971

Best-selling single – *My Sweet Lord*, George Harrison. A champion of the age, on account of his Concert for Bangladesh (remember Eric Clapton, Bob Dylan and someone calling himself Leon Russell?)
Best-selling album – *Bridge Over Troubled Water*, Simon & Garfunkel. Not a misprint.

1972

Best-selling single – *Amazing Grace*, Royal Scots Dragoon Guards Band. Kilts and wind.
Best-selling album – *20 Dynamic Hits*, Various Artists. Shoddy stuff.

1973

Best-selling single – *Tie A Yellow Ribbon*, Dawn. Yes, this one. Dah dah dah dah dah dah dah dah daah daah dee.
Best-selling album – *Aladdin Sane*, David Bowie. Suck, baby suck, etc.

1974

Best-selling single – *Tiger Feet*, Mud. A virtuoso display. Pablo Casals unfortunately died (1973) before he could hear it.
Best-selling album – *The Singles 1969–1973*, The Carpenters. The thin girl, and was it her brother?

1975
Best-selling single – *Bye Bye Baby*, The Bay City Rollers. We are all to blame in some way.
Best-selling album – *Best of the Stylistics*, The Stylistics. What did you expect? Miles Davis?

1976
Best-selling single – *Save Your Kisses For Me*, Brotherhood of Man. A tax write-off.
Best-selling album – *Greatest Hits*, ABBA. Rather like mainlining on toothpaste, we are told.

1977
Best-selling single – *Don't give up on us*, David Soul. Really. The power of television.
Best-selling album – *Arrival*, ABBA.

You probably thought everything had changed by now. Well, it hadn't.

1978
Best-selling single – *Rivers of Babylon/ Brown Girl in the Ring*, Boney M. This was the one that shamed you on holiday.
Best-selling album – *Saturday Night Fever*, Various Artists. And stretch, two three, and point, two three, and *down*, and *up*, and *turn*, and . . . are you all right?

1979
Best-selling single – *Bright Eyes*, Art Garfunkel. Something to do with rabbits and haemorrhoids.
Best-selling album – *Parallel Lines*, Blondie. Get your hair cut!

21

Work and nostalgia

Whatever else we do now, we almost certainly work. We have to: we need the money. Quite often, our dependants need our money.

Not only that, but we have also *become* our work in many ways. Just as we might have black hair and brown eyes, we bear the characteristics of our job. We've been doing it so long now (a good ten years, maybe) that we have turned into what we do. We *are* corporate directors – gregarious, shifty, a little dull; or doctors – placid, reassuring, secretive; or designers – harassed, passionate,

loquacious. What we think of as *us* has been fashioned by the years of work.

At the same time, work is a discrete activity for most of us. We don't work all the time, unless we're driven obsessives. We try to keep a part of our lives for something else – to which we give a name such as Recreation or Sport or Being a Mother to the Children or just Being about the House. This is time which isn't like work time. There are different alliances, different rewards, different problems.

But our work selves intrude. How

HAVING A RECREATION IS IMPORTANT. ONE'S BOUND TO GET A WHO'S WHO ENTRY BEFORE LONG.

FOR NEW IDEAS*

ON OFFICE COPYING

the moment when we can stop.

Work has, however, taken away the identity we had before. This identity was usually something fashioned at school, or in college. Was it any more true to our ideas of ourselves than the one we bear now? It doesn't matter. We still feel a nostalgia. We're brought up short when we recollect what we used to know – useless knowledge, if we work in an ad agency or a civil engineer's office, the mere residue of an undirected education – but knowledge which is still appealing, for all its uselessness. We remember how fresh experiences were then, when we were different. We think of how un-routine things were.

could they not? We spend a decade conditioning ourselves to act in a certain way, with a certain decisiveness, caution, thoroughness, and the result is that we can't shake it off at half past six and revert to some more natural state. So we busy ourselves about the house or go on holiday in much the same way as we do our jobs.

And this is fine. It doesn't matter. One way of doing things is probably not much worse than another. As long as nobody gets hurt, we can get through life tolerably well this way.

But at the back of our minds, we know that something isn't right. We know that the job has sharpened some of our talents and even given us other, quite new ones; we experience a number of pleasurable sensations at work – labouring successfully under pressure, completing the job on time, the anticipation of

'He likes the work itself, too. 'He likes the sense of working against limitations, of seeing what kind of mountain shape can be developed given certain unalterable geological and meteorological data. And then the sudden lurching shift of perspective, the falling through the bottom of things, when you discover that these constants have been or could be altered after all. 'He likes the way they suddenly drop the whole interlocking tangle of folding and faulting and erosion, and stroll round for lunch in the pub they've adopted. 'He likes the smell of dust in the office, and the smell of clean white shirts as the sweat begins to come through the armpits.'

Michael Frayn, *Sweet Dreams*

23

So what do we do? It's now, in our thirties, that we look for change. No longer in the forties, as popular mythology has it (its given name: The Mid-Life Crisis), but now. Material prosperity increases; we enjoy now what the previous generation enjoyed in its forties. We even, it seems, get promoted earlier, as the nature of work and of the work structure change. We get a lot of what we're working for, right now.

So what do we do, to change? Many women decide to get pregnant. We might get divorced. Sometimes we walk out of our jobs. Sometimes we go to university, or go back to university. Maybe we up sticks and move to another, better part of the country to *cool out*. Sometimes we just look for something to do which isn't work or bringing the children up (which is of course work, but without cash payment) or sleeping or watching the TV or shopping. Something which is not necessary, but is worth doing. A *hobby*, in other words.

Now is the time when we discover, sometimes to our own surprise, that we have *interests*. If asked to complete an entry in *Who's Who* we might wind up with 'Walking; gardening; wine-making; opera; sleeping' without even knowing how these things became *interests*.

 HOBBIES

You think you might have a *hobby*, but are too *embarrassed* to tell anyone about it? Compare your *leisure activities* with those of the *great*, and see if you really are a *hobbied person*.

BRANAGH, Kenneth Charles: 'Reading, playing guitar.'

COE, Sebastian Newbold: 'Listening to recorded or preferably live jazz, theatre, reading.'

KENNEDY, Nigel Paul: 'Golf, football (watching & playing).'

MOYNIHAN, the Hon. Colin Berkeley: 'Collecting Nonesuch books, music, sport.'

Hobbies, a brief bibliography:
Practical Taxidermy and Home Decoration, Joseph H. Batty (Orange Judd, 1880)
Teach Yourself Alcoholism, Meier Glatt (Teach Yourself Books, 1975)
Let's Make Some Undies, Marion Hall (W. Foulsham & Co., 1954)
Fun With Knotting String, Heidy Willsmore (Kaye & Ward, 1977)
The Mystery of Golf, Theodore Arnold Haultain (Macmillan, 1910)

Once, we looked down on people with interests, with *hobbies*. When we were in our twenties, we thought that life was full enough just thinking about ourselves in those long periods of freedom that the twenties offered, without having to fill them up with anything else. Now, we are far busier people, busy almost to the point of hysteria. And yet we have *hobbies*, on top of it all. Don't we? Ask yourself: what do *you* do, when all the essential tasks are over?

What we believe

DIALOGUE THE FIRST: THE TRANSCENDENTAL

It is the fourth day before the winter solstice, and **JILL** and **REBECCA** are sitting by the fire of **REBECCA**'s home. They are discussing the nature of mysticism and belief.

JILL: Without religion, man is no more than a form of brute beast. It is that, more than the power of abstract reasoning, which elevates us above the kine and the denizens of the deep. You may know a man by his Christianity.

REBECCA: In truth, so I believed myself. But now, no longer.

JILL: Why, then – was there a falling-away from faith?

REBECCA: Not a falling-away from faith, but a falling-away from faith in Christianity.

JILL: Why so? Is not the Christian church a church for all men, for all time? And is not the Church of England the best of all Christian churches?

REBECCA: No, indeed.

JILL: Tell me your reasons.

REBECCA: In the first case, the Church of England is a conservative church. It is a church whose authority lies in its age and its preservation of a form of worship which can be traced back through two millennia. Its answers to new problems tend to be old answers – answers which have answered other questions in the past, and which will answer other questions in the future. I found this stifling. In the second case, the vicar changed.

JILL: In what way did he change?

REBECCA: He became a new vicar. The previous vicar installed a seventeenth-century liturgy and called Family Communion,

Mass, pronounced *Marce*. This was both moving and rather glamorous. The new vicar liked to speak as one of the people. He enjoyed playing a kazoo in the pulpit. His cheese 'n' absinthe mingles drove many away. I am not alone in this. Since 1970, the Church of England has lost nearly one million active members.

✳   ✳   ✳

For if he that cometh preacheth another Jesus, whom we have not preached, or if ye receive another spirit, which ye have not received, or another gospel, which ye have not accepted, ye might well bear with him.

For I suppose I was not a whit behind the very chiefest apostles.

But though I be rude in speech, yet not in knowledge; but we have been thoroughly made manifest among you in all things.

2 Corinthians, chapter 11, verses 4–6

For if someone comes to you and preaches a Jesus other than the Jesus we preached, or if you receive a different spirit from the one you received, or a different gospel from the one you accepted, you put up with it easily enough.

But I do not think I am in the least inferior to those 'super-apostles'.

I may not be a trained speaker, but I do have knowledge. We have made this perfectly clear to you in every way.

New International Version (1973)

JILL: And is this why you are now living in an abandoned farm building near Glastonbury, in Somerset?

REBECCA: I came here by many paths.

JILL: What was the first path?

REBECCA: After leaving the Christian church, I tried holistic massage. That was the first path. Then I tried aromatherapy for my urethritis. Then I experimented with T'Ai Chi. Then Hinduism. Then Hinduism and yoga. Then Zen Shiatsu. Then Buddhism. Then Gurdjieff Ouspensky. Then I went into therapy for a while. Then I trained as an astrologer, but couldn't get the hang, quite. Then I tried Transcendental Meditation with the Maharishi Mahesh Yogi. Then I became a Maoist. Then I tried Floating. Then I had to go to hospital for a while. Finally, I left hospital and joined a community near Banbury in Oxfordshire, most of which disbanded while the remainder came here to Glastonbury. I am now, broadly speaking, an earth-worshipper with primitive Christian overtones and a keen interest in standing stones, the Tarot, the I-Ching and God as a Woman.

JILL: So many different paths?

REBECCA: And so costly.

JILL: How, costly?

REBECCA: A flotation session costs the best part of £25, and they recommend that you have three sessions, to get the benefit. Then there's an alpha-waves stimulator, around £300. An energy plate's £20, and even a crystal pendant can go over £25.

JILL: Mum's awfully worried about you.

'What a relief to be able to relax and play/work, for the first time in a large gathering, with a peer group of equals. There was no need to confront dominant leaders. The facilitation truly came out of the group. There was a feeling of commitment to the process of learning the new way, which is probably a very old way, practised in the stone circles of the ancient ones.

'I experienced a space in which people contributed their unique perspectives, suggestions and inspirations. There was one moment when someone proposed "I think we should have a facilitator for this bit," and we just listened and passed it by, on with our journey into the delicious unknown.'

Ann, writing in the *Glastonbury Communicator*, issue no. 7

REBECCA: It is I who should be worrying about Mum.

JILL: Why is that?

REBECCA: Because Mum has chosen the path of The World. I have chosen the path of The Earth.

JILL: She thinks thirty-seven is a bit late to leave it.

REBECCA: I am entering my most creative time. At least I've stopped going to church.

JILL: I wish you hadn't.

REBECCA: Well, what is the point of the C of E? What does it do for you?

JILL: It is a still point in a changing world. Its ritual, however phrased, is what makes it worth doing. What you find stifling, I find refreshing.

REBECCA: Do you believe in the Resurrection? Do you believe in the Virgin Birth? Do you believe in the truth of the Gospels? Do you believe in these things as sincerely as you believe in the existence of your Renault estate car?

JILL: Not in the same way.

REBECCA: How *do* you believe in them, then?

JILL: I can't say.

REBECCA: Do you believe in them at all?

JILL: Well, yes.

REBECCA: Or do you believe in the act of Going to Church? Do you like to be there because other people like to be there? Because it fits in with the way you see yourself? Because you can't live without doing the proper thing? Like Mum?

JILL: I'd rather be a paid-up churchgoer with a sense of pride in myself and my family than a part-time schizophrenic who lives her life in a fog of garbled third-hand mysticism and a building that houses goats, chickens and, from the feel of it, fleas like small sharks.

REBECCA: That is your way. This is mine. My way is to change, to invent, to synthesize.

JILL: You make it up as you go along.

REBECCA: Is there something wrong with that?

JILL: Where's it going?

REBECCA: Does it have to go somewhere?

JILL: I'm going to Heaven.

REBECCA: What is your proof?

JILL: I might be going to Heaven.

REBECCA: Well, I'm going to the pub. Coming?

JILL: No, I've got to get back. We're going out to dinner.

Unmarried Sex

Problems? Personal problems? Love problems? TELL CONSUELA . . .

Dear Consuela,

I am thirty-four years old, single and free. I have a good job, a flat, a car, a mortgage, I take at least one holiday abroad every year, I have plenty of friends, life is full of possibilities. What is the matter with me?

Sue

(Did I say thirty-four? That's a lie, I'm thirty-five. *Just* thirty-five.)

Dear Consuela,

No, I'm not plain. I'm perfectly nice-looking. I admit, the figure's gone a bit, but then it started going when I was still twenty-five. And, yes, there are a couple of lines around the eyes, and a grey hair or twenty (at least they're all together in a neat bunch, not lurking about all over the place) and the neck doesn't look too good in some, particularly unflattering, lights, but then I don't suppose yours would, either. I also get a bit shrill sometimes. Sorry about that. Basically, I just seem to have lost the knack with men. I mean, no boyfriend, no *regular* boyfriend, for four years. Which is a long time to go without It.

Sue

CONSUELA WRITES:
Dear Sue: I don't think you're being frank. You make everything sound rosy, then you say that something's the matter. How can I help if you're not straight with me? Are you holding something back? Are you, for instance, appallingly plain?

CONSUELA WRITES:

While I understand your difficulties, Sue, it seems to me that you're being defeatist. What about your friends? Are they all married men? Or are they all female? Don't you go to parties where you can meet new people? And what about work? You said that you have a good job – doesn't it bring you into contact with all sorts? And failing that, have you ever thought of joining a club for single people? There are some very good ones around. They organize social and sporting events, weekends away and holiday trips.

They're low-key, fun and there's no pressure to pair anyone off. I shall send you the literature by return.

Dear Consuela,

Yes, yes, no, no, NO.

Sue

Things happen after a Badedas bath

Sophie

CONSUELA WRITES:

Dear Richard: I don't think you're being frank. You make everything sound rosy, then you say that it's awful. How can I help if you're not straight with me? Are you holding something back? Are you, for instance, appallingly plain?

Dear Consuela,

I am thirty-six years old, unmarried, I have a good job, a car, a flat, plenty of friends, I take plenty of holidays abroad, and I've had plenty of girlfriends in my time. Unfortunately, the supply seems to have dried up. I don't know why. I can't put my finger on it. Two-thirds of my male friends have got married, and the rest of us just sit around in the pub all weekend. Having fun. It's awful.

Richard

CONSUELA WRITES:
It does strike me as strange. I get letters from single women bemoaning the absence of men; and from single men bemoaning the absence of women. What's the matter with you? Why are you sitting around complaining – when all you have to do is get up, introduce yourselves, and start something new? I know we all get a bit stuck in our ways once we're over thirty, but for Heaven's sake, isn't it worth a try?

Dear Consuela,

Yes, I am appallingly plain. But that's not supposed to matter with men. And I've had at least three real girlfriends, so there must be more to me than bad skin, frizzy hair and a slouch. I've got a nice personality, I'm considerate in bed (at least I was), I wash every day. To be frank, there wasn't a shortage ten years ago. But ever since the good men started to go down and get married and have families and I don't know what . . . well, I don't know what.

Richard

Dear Consuela,

Since you mention it, some of us do get up and try. In fact, I feel sure I've tried with your correspondent Richard, or someone very like him. You try with Richard. You'll find that not only is he no oil-painting (more like The Picture of Dorian Gray), but he's dull, predictable, lacklustre, hidebound, sexist and clumsy. I need someone either much younger, or much older.

Sue

CONSUELA WRITES:
That's all very well, Sue . . .

NOW WE ARE THIRTYSOMETHING

Dear Consuela,

Hold on. If that's the Sue I once bought a drink for – out of pity – in a certain low-rent wine bar she frequents (Naughty Nineties postcards in brass frames and scrums of desperate shrieking middle-aged women hogging the tables), then I don't think she's telling the full story. I'm not surprised she's gone short for four years. She's *ghastly*. Typically enough, being a woman, she heaps the blame on me. Well, it's time we men stood

up for ourselves. I for one am going to go after much younger women because they're tractable, cute, and society tacitly approves of that sort of thing. Sue can fetch up with some young twat if she wants to, but I think he'll have to be desperate as well. More chance with an octogenarian. There are plenty about.

Richard.

I'M A WOMAN IN MY THIRTIES but age hasn't blunted my passion for all things: books, cinema, wine, travel, conversation and good living. Is there a man out there with more to him than just the change in his pockets? Box E8132

Dear Consuela,

This may sound ridiculous, but I have recently met a very nice man, the same age as me, similar tastes, sense of humour, not exactly good-looking but perfectly presentable, and I'm wondering whether or not I should marry him. Don't laugh. I know I'm in my mid thirties and ought to know my own mind by now, but I'm scared of the commitment. Having lived on my own for four years, I've found ways of doing things that *I* like, on my own, without having to bother about anyone else, and now I've met this man, it means shaking everything up. Is it worth it?

Sue

SMART GRADUATE MALE seeks bright, personable, attractive female, 25–35, for fun, travel, theatre, maybe more? Photo guarantees reply. Box E5467

CONSUELA WRITES:
If you're that abusive cow who wrote a few weeks back, then you can drop dead for all I care.

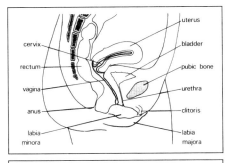

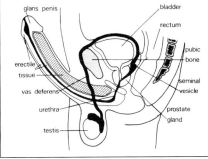

Dear Consuela,

I have met this terrific woman and I want to marry her. The thing is, we met through the Lonely Hearts ads and I'm afraid my friends will laugh at me when they find out. What can I do?

Richard

CONSUELA WRITES:
You think your *friends* will laugh at you? Let's *all* have a laugh: I'm going to suspend my regular practice of not naming the derelicts who write in to this page, and tell the world that your full name is

Richard Whittenstall
Flat 6
Dascombe Mansions
Cheveley Road
Manchester M0 7RD

That's dealt with that little problem.

Dear Consuela,

Look: sorry about that. But you'd feel the same if you were my age, the biological clock ticking away – I mean, I'd like to have children . . .

CONSUELA WRITES:
I've had three kids and two divorces, and if you think it's made me happy, then think again. And if you don't care much for being in your thirties, wait until the forties. You want clinical depression? I can give you clinical depression.

MATURE AGONY AUNT seeks uncomplicated relationship with anyone male or female, age unimportant, everything unimportant, but please no critics. I have recently lost my job, so please no critics. I just can't take it right now. Box B35467.

Frazzled on Mahe Island

1 So it was a toss-up between this one

'A sweeping white beach fringed with date palms and oleanders . . . a sea so blue, you'll think it was made in Heaven . . . luxury five-star accommodation, with a bar that reaches down to the water's edge, and an internationally-famed restaurant where the food is as sensational as the setting . . .

Sounds too good to be true? Think again! This fabulous resort, a mere twenty minutes from the recently-opened Holdana International Airport, offers you everything you could want from a holiday – and more!

As well as beautiful surroundings, it has everything for the more active holidaymaker: scuba diving, dinghy sailing, paragliding, riding, microliting, golf, judo classes, shark-fishing, tennis, all-in wrestling, a fully-equipped gym and a banked motor racing track engineered for speeds up to 200 mph. Children are welcomed, and there's a daily nursery plus round-the-clock babysitting and nanny care. The Kids' Mini-Fair (for five-year-olds and over) offers an advanced playground, horse-riding, miniature tennis and a gun club.

And in the evenings? Well, why not kick off with a long tropical cocktail in Trader Sam's beach bar – freshly picked fruits, a tall glass, a cascade of ice, and a healthy splash of something a little stronger! Soon it'll be time to take a long, hard look at tonight's menu . . . what'll it be? Swordfish grilled over charcoal? *Noisettes* of lamb with a *coulis* of limes and paw-paw? Or how about *stakoo* – a delicious stew made from a small local furry creature?

Then – just linger over your coffee and liqueurs and watch the stars come out (maybe you'll catch a falling one!) – or if you're in the mood, follow your ears (you'll be hard pressed not to!) and make your way to one of the liveliest and most action-packed nightclubs this side of Manhattan – Sango's Place! Seven nights a week, from eight 'til late, Sango plays the sounds you want to hear, and dispenses his own unique brand of hospitality at Sango's Bar. Don't plan on an early start next morning once you've found Sango's! This one's definitely not for the faint-hearted – ask Sango!'

Club Maquis Summer Holiday brochure, courtesy Smooth Obfuscations plc, the leading tourism PR group

and this one

SEYCHELLES – Discreet pleasure in tropical paradise, Mahe. No children. Leatherhead 29786.

Courtesy *The Times* classifieds

Matty and Chris examined their bank accounts. *Club Maquis* was £750 a head for fourteen nights, B & B. The Seychelles were £1500 a head for fourteen nights, half-board. Well, no one was going to call *them* cheapskates even if it meant staying at home for the rest of the decade.

2 Not so simple: when to go?

Evidently not late June, July, August or early September on account of the depravities of the school holidays.

Beastly French children crapping on the beach, rough, pathetic English families fighting gloomily over the carousel at the airport, that kind of thing. May, early June, second half September. Or is it different in the Indian Ocean?

But Chris has a four-day conference on 7 June, and Matty has to go to Malmö to examine a machine that cleans deep-fat fryers on 2 June. Second half of June, then, Damn. Hope no kids. As advertised.

3 Is that okay with you?

Matty runs into small problems with Dave from within the department, who claims to have booked two sun-kissed weeks in Miami at around the same time. Teresa, whose accounting section has to liaise with both of them, has already paid the balance on a Far Eastern round trip taking in Hong Kong, Bangkok, Singapore, Bali, Jakarta, Brunei and Penang. Laurence, her partner in the accounting section, actually has the flight tickets for his trip to Jamaica. Keith, the department head, is keeping quiet, but makes it plain that the second half of June is his, arguably having something to do with his secretary, Debbie, and a certain destination in Latin America.

After three days of sniping and gratuitous pettiness, they allow Matty the very beginning of June or the very end. Particularly irritating, since no one seems even half interested in the extravagance or exoticism of The Seychelles. The problem is resolved when Chris announces that his conference has been put forward to 5 June, although something in his manner suggests to Matty that he got the date wrong in the first place.

4 Leaving.

Chris attempts to clear his desk by jamming all outstanding items in the biggest, bottom drawer. Matty attempts to clear her desk by doing two weeks' work in three days.

This means that she is up at two-thirty in the morning, ironing small items of foreign clothing, while the plane is due to leave Gatwick at ten-thirty.

A survey done by Barclaycard revealed that of the 20 million British tourists who go abroad every year for their holidays:

- One in three takes a supply of teabags
- One in five takes a roll of lavatory paper
- One in ten takes a favourite dressing gown
- One in twenty takes his/her own pillow
- One woman in twenty takes a cuddly toy
- One man in seventy-eight takes a cuddly toy

This means that she falls asleep in the car on the way to the airport and cannot be woken except by a party of electricians returning from Corfu, who put her in a baggage trolley and push her the length of the terminal building at speeds of up to fifteen miles per hour. As she comes to, outside the duty-free wristwatches, it suddenly occurs to her that she's only ever had one holiday with Chris before, and that was three days in northern France. She thinks: I don't know this bloke at all.

5 Arriving.

'. . . Delighted to see you, Mr and Mrs White – Dartmouth, I'm sorry – not married yet, ha, ha, two weeks in paradise and you will be, we can arrange a beautiful and tasteful ceremony at sunset on the jetty just behind the oil tanks – this is the Captain's lounge bar, this is the Captain himself – buy him a rum and he'll tell you his life story in four different languages, two of them English – and this is the staircase – can I give you a hand with that bag? You okay? You look a bit red. Yes, it's a long flight, thirteen hours, and the delay of course, well it's a problem getting the parts . . . watch out for that spider, yes they do bite, but they're very rarely fatal, no, termites are relatively harmless, you saw the mound in the garden did you? This is your room, hello, we'll have to fix that bulb, may I ask you not to flush the toilet between the hours of eleven at night and seven in the morning while the sanitation

department is still in, don't be alarmed, cockroaches are a way of life in this part of the world, the gekkos are friendly too, although they won't eat the spiders. Tomorrow morning may I invite you to a complimentary breakfast of tinned yam, tinned pineapple, tinned paw-paw, Belgian coffee, German rolls, Swiss sugar and English butter processed and packed in Kenya? We can't grow these things ourselves, yet, you see. Apart from nutmegs. Do you like nutmegs?'

6 Postcards.

OBVERSE: Great bulging granite formations topped with palms, azure sea melting over coral reef, dazzling white sands, laughing piccaninnies dancing in shade of passion-fruit plant, man attempting to fix broken Mini-Moke, bottom left (next to oil dump).

REVERSE: Weather stunning, food great, Chris has found some snorkelling gear and now I can't get him out of the water! Got a bit grazed on the coral, but the national health service here better than at home! We'll bring you back a spider – we found one in our bed the size of an LP!

OBVERSE: View of Victoria (capital of Mahe) with miniature Big Ben lookalike clock at crossroads. Deserted roads, blinding heat, palm trees, covered stalls selling gourd-like wooden seed pods carved into fruit bowls, ashtrays, chessboards,

punchbowls. Lovable gnarled mulatto waves Friendly Greeting, while tourists trudge from branch of Barclays Bank (Seychelles branch) clutching thick wads of local currency.

REVERSE: Wonderful time being had by all (despite Chris's tummy). Sunsets quite spectacular. Chris bumped his head again while snorkelling and now has rather an impressive bandage! Jacques Cousteau he's not! I'm as brown as a local. Who cares about ageing in the sun? I love it!

OBVERSE: Snapshot of the Coco-de-Mer, an extremely mysterious fruit that looks like a part of the female body and grows only on one island in the Seychelles group. Hairy cleft.

REVERSE: No rude language please!

7 Returning.

Matty and Chris's return flight is held up for seven hours. They have spent all their money on gewgaws and revolting tinned restaurant meals. They are not speaking to each other, following a disagreement on the eighth night over whether or not Chris was going to have a *third* bottle of wine with dinner. He did. This disagreement led to a reconciliation on the tenth morning

THE BOOKS YOU ACTUALLY READ ON HOLIDAY:

Rivals,
Jilly Cooper
Rock Star,
Jackie Collins
The Day Of The Jackal,
Frederick Forsyth (again)
Alex: Magnum Force,
Charles Peattie and Russell Taylor
The True Adventures Of The Rolling Stones,
Stanley Booth
The Book Of Daily Mail Crosswords

THE BOOKS YOU MEAN TO READ ON HOLIDAY:

A La Recherche Du Temps Perdu,
Marcel Proust (*in the Penguin translation*)
One Hundred Years Of Solitude,
Gabriel García Márquez (*in the Picador translation*)
A Brief History Of Time,
Stephen Hawking
Hotel Du Lac,
Anita Brookner
Ulysses,
James Joyce
Eminent Victorians,
Lytton Strachey
Seven Pillars Of Wisdom,
T. E. Lawrence
Mani,
Patrick Leigh Fermor
Flaubert's Parrot,
Julian Barnes

culminating in a bout of furious unaccustomed holiday sex (the kind you don't get anywhere else), which in turn led them to wander onto the beach much later in the day, feeling sheepish and rather pleased with themselves. This happy condition disintegrated on the eleventh night when Matty described Chris as vulgar, selfish, childish and dull, while he described her as self-righteous, holier-than-thou and hypocritical. The start of this disagreement? Chris's inability (or cussed refusal) to bottle up his farts in the hotel bedroom. This has been a source of conflict since day three of their relationship. In the uneasy perfection of paradise island, it now gets out of hand. They lose a night's

IT'S THAT DAMNED APPLE THING YOU PERSUADED ME TO EAT.

sleep, slugging it out. All the good of the holiday (holiday sleep: the kind you don't get anywhere else) is promptly undone.

Now they wait amid property speculators and TV celebrities who went out with them but stayed somewhere smarter, and negligent Seychellois airport operatives, for a new engine to be fixed to their Airbus. They will arrive at Gatwick in the small hours, brown, fit and furious.

. . . Women say their partners have unpleasant habits, many of which interfere with lovemaking, such as 'burping', 'breaking wind', scratching', 'snorting with catarrh', smoking ('I wish he would give up smoking. I can smell the faggy smell even when he has brushed his teeth a couple of time and rinsed with mouthwash') and drinking ('If my husband has been drinking I don't like to kiss him because he has stale breath'). A little self-reflection about such matters may be even more important for some men than improving sexual techniques . . .

Woman's Experience of Sex,
Sheila Kitzinger

45

Marriage for the over-thirties

A CONSUMERS' GUIDE

1 The Rational:

FEATURES:	Register Office, handful of guests, parents optional, drink-up at couple's house (in which they've been living for several years already). Clothes: mufti, plus carnation for groom; small bouquet for bride. Honeymoon not essential, and anyway (a) difficult to fit in with all those meetings (b) not much different from your annual holiday. Also useful for couples who've had children before getting married. Short Register Office ceremony saves on baby-sitting fees.
DRAWBACKS:	A trifle joyless.
RINGS:	Optional. Not usually worn by either party.
COST:	Minimal.
GUARANTEE:	1–5 years. Infidelity likely, but does not invalidate marriage.
VERDICT:	Handy for determined sceptics, ex-members of the Socialist Workers Party, liberal intellectuals who want it to be known that there are more important things in life than just getting a green certificate.

2 The Rational de Luxe, or Semi-Rational

FEATURES: Register Office, as for The Rational, but with the following additional extras: parents of bride and groom (if living); blessing in church afterwards (if either spouse already divorced, or if neither party can agree on going the whole way in a church wedding); any children born pre-union can also be baptised in a job lot, along with the blessing; more guests and consequently, bigger knees-up at the couple's home (or even in a hired room; marquees are not supplied with this model).

DRAWBACKS: A bit complicated: you have to get a hard core of guests and relatives over to the Register Office first; then rendezvous at the church; then get back to the drink-up. People tend to get lost, and fights can break out. You also have nearly as much administrative bother as a full wedding (see The Traditional) without all the pomp.

RINGS: Likely for both bride and groom.

COST: Varies: much as for The Rational if you have the binge in your own home and don't serve champagne; but can go through the roof if you hire a restaurant and insist on Moët all the way through.

GUARANTEE: 5 years, with an extra 5 years optional cover. If children already present at marriage, guarantee can be extended for further 10 years.

VERDICT: Essentially something of a compromise. Often the result of one partner badgering the other into making a bit of a show. Likely among youngish thirties types who nonetheless feel too old for The Traditional.

3 The Traditional

FEATURES:	Church service, guests, parents, binge afterwards in hired accommodation of some kind. Bride will wear something special for the occasion, but not the full fig with veil. Groom will buy a smart suit. Speeches after the ceremony (although best man/bride's father not essential; speeches more likely to be made by bride and groom themselves – they're old enough, after all). Children unlikely (although bride may well be pregnant). Wedding may coincide with the couple flogging their separate flats and buying a three-bedroom house somewhere. Official honeymoon probable. Popular with those who've found romance late in life, and would like to make up for those lost years. Sometimes an impulse purchase.
DRAWBACKS:	No more than for any other trad. wedding.
RINGS:	Certainly for the bride; optional for the groom (trad. males may prefer to keep to the old proprietorial ways).
COST:	Stiff, but at least there's no bridal gown, going-away dress or morning suit to buy. Equally, the couple may not be able to ask the parents for a hand-out if they're doing it largely for their own satisfaction.
GUARANTEE:	5 years, minimum, renewable every two years by negotiation.
VERDICT:	A bit sentimental (let's face it, two 35-year-olds mooching down the aisle are hardly embarking on life's first great adventure) but pleasant enough. Can lead to cynical objections from users of The Rational; can also spark resentment from those who've purchased a Rational de Luxe. (Why couldn't *we* have done it *properly*?)

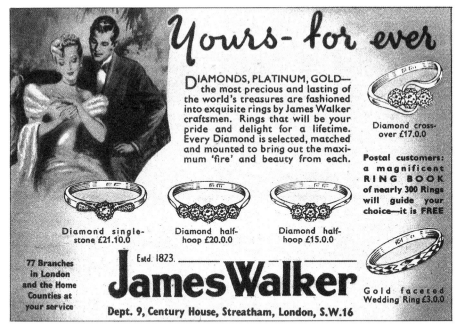

HARMONY before MATRIMONY.

49

4 The Preposterous

FEATURES: Full (very full) church service; flowers, engraved invitations, gargantuan cake, going-away dress, etc. Groom may feel obliged to ask bride's father's permission for bride's hand. Father may feel obliged to pay for part of the event. Full bridal gear, plus veil; groom in bought/rented morning suit (possibly belonging to other male member of family, if traditional household). Hundreds and hundreds of guests. Marquee, live music, best man (someone at college with groom, or if college friendships now too dilapidated to call upon, partner from work). Honeymoon somewhere thousands of miles away. Popular with older men marrying women in their twenties – still young enough to be entitled to a proper send-off.

DRAWBACKS: Groom (if much more than ten years older than bride) can look a bit of a Lothario as he escorts her down the aisle. Equally, if both parties in their thirties, both can look merely desperate. Likely to draw criticisms of bad taste from users of Rational and Traditional models (although Semi-Rational users more likely to express mixed envy and scorn, as above). Rather out of step with peers and colleagues (many of whom will be divorced by now, anyway) even though the age at which people get married is rising.

RINGS: All round, plus massive engagement ring for bride.

COST: Nightmarish.

GUARANTEE: 6–12 months. Non-renewable. Infidelity indemnity essential (cash only).

VERDICT: For determined consumers.

5 The Insane, or Showbiz

FEATURES: Wedding on a boat/in a cellar/on the stage of the Garrick Theatre, London/up a mountain/in a bothy/on the top of a bus/in the couple's front room. Parents, guests, priest, etc. entirely optional. Marriage may not be legal. Showbiz types/gangsters/self-made millionaires/journalists/crazed hippies/Americans most likely purchasers.

DRAWBACKS: None.

RINGS: As many or as few as desired.

COST: Not relevant.

GUARANTEE: None offered.

VERDICT: Make sure the News Desk can fit you in before going ahead.

Homes and gardens

From *Homes & Gardens*:

. . . The moment Sally and Peter Herbert saw the nineteenth-century, four-bedroomed terraced house, they knew they had to have it. 'It was love at first sight', confesses Sally. 'Something about it spoke to us.'

It stands in a charming enclave of similar houses in the heart of increasingly fashionable Deptford which has mercifully escaped the ravages of Sixties property developers and Seventies road schemes. Within, however, all was not well.

'Basically, the previous owners had messed it about with no idea of period style or taste', says Peter. 'There were coal-effect gas fires in the living-rooms; the bathroom was covered in cork tiles, floor to ceiling; the kitchen had been knocked through into a disastrous tunnel lined with Melamine; and the roof had been re-tiled in the most revolting red pantiles instead of black slates. There was also a terrible old glass lean-to at the back, used for growing tomatoes and courgettes.'

But Sally and Peter are nothing if not resourceful, and with the aid of

> Mintel, the consumer trend watchers, claim that consumer spending on DIY and garden products has gone up by 96 per cent between 1983 and 1989; while spending on furniture and furnishings has increased by 52 per cent in the same period.

some good friends in the building and design world they soon set to work to transform this town house into a haven of beauty and calm. Their first task was to rebuild the wall which divided the front room from the back parlour.

'At first we tried breeze blocks,' Sally explains, 'but it very quickly occurred to us that the only way was to do it properly, using original bricks.' Damian ffrench-Farce, their 'brilliant, totally undiscovered' interior designer, scoured dozens of builders' yards, hunting down just the right sort of town-house brick, thrown out in the course of demolishing other houses of similar vintage; when the supply ran out, bricks were made specially for them by local craftsmen. 'There was a shade of pink which we had to get, or the whole thing would have looked wrong. Then, of course, we

Ask any AGA owner!

REGD. TRADE MARK

Can you really do every kind of cooking that there is?

Open one of the Aga ovens. Lift up the lid of one of the Aga hotplates. Do this any time of the day or night; and there, straight away, without a second's delay, is exactly the heat you want. That's what thermostat control does: you don't need a griller or boiler or any other 'help-out' when you've an Aga.

Can you do all the cooking and heat all your water, all for (about) 1/- a day?

However much you use it (even if you cook right through the night) the Aga cannot possibly use more than 3¼ tons of fuel in a year. And the fuel is coke—easy to come by, all the year round.

Can you boil a 4-pint kettle of cold water in 4 minutes?

The Aga boiling plate is the fastest you can get. Fast heat is what gives jam its colour, keeps green vegetables green and fried food crisp.

Can you cook an egg-thickened sauce without 'catching' it, ever?

As gently as you like. Simmering heat is controlled, always: it cannot 'run away'.

Can you make tough meat tender? Can you keep hot meals hot without spoiling? Can you cook ham, stock, porridge, through the night?

The Aga can—with its simmering oven. This is the best-beloved thing about this best-beloved cooker of all.

Can you bake cakes that are never 'sad', roast meat that is never unevenly done?

The Aga oven is made of solid cast iron, which throws out really *penetrating* heat—as the old brick baker's oven did; and it's steady heat too.

Can you boil fast (really fast)? Can you simmer gently (really gently)?

The boiling plate and simmering plate are *separate*, and each is big enough to take three 8-pint saucepans at a time.

Can your cooker keep the kitchen warm in winter without making it too hot in summer?

The Aga is insulated. Just enough heat gets out . . . the kitchen is always 'just right'. What a comfort that is on a cold and frosty morning! (The fire is alight, of course: the Aga need never go out.)

★Besides all this, the Aga offers you Hire Purchase over five years, and a cast-iron guarantee for ten. H.P. can cost as little as ¿2 a month. The Aga is not 'for princes and rich men only'—no, indeed. It is for people who want to SAVE money.

Now then! Find out all about the other wonderful things the Aga does. The leaflets are detailed, interesting, full of facts and figures. There's nothing to pay and, of course, 'no obligation'.

The best thing would be to write off NOW, this minute. If you can't, fold over the corner of the page or tie a knot in your handkerchief so you don't forget.

This is the address:

AGA HEAT LTD.

2/22 Orchard House,
Orchard Street, London, W.1

Proprietors: Allied Ironfounders Ltd.
Makers of
cookers, boilers and fires.

had to plaster it using the right kind of plaster.'

Meanwhile, the kitchen was being gutted and an architect friend drew up an entirely new conception for the space, involving limed Spanish oak, wrought-iron brackets (many bought at David de Spenceley's antiques salvage warehouse in Fulham) and 300-watt pinpoints of light hidden in the ceiling.

'At first, we thought it would be too beautiful to use,' admitted Peter, 'but we accustomed ourselves to its ways.' Among the design features are a self-emptying rubbish bin with an intricate hinge mechanism; a two-level three-stage fan-assisted microwave on a chest-high swivel, which can be concealed in a malachite unit; and the figure of a negro slave, carved out of ironwood, which is in fact the cold tap on the kitchen sink.

Upstairs there were more problems. A mousse-pink suite occupied the bathroom, while the bedrooms were lined with cheap DIY cupboards. Damian cleared the whole floor and, in an inspired move, installed a coke-fired stove snatched from a derelict BR waiting room. This magnificent beast stands six feet high and requires almost constant stoking. 'But it's worth it', argues Peter. 'It's so much more *real* than a gas boiler. It's a living thing. And it makes the most fantastic hot water.' Just Splashes, of Richmond, Yorkshire, supplied an iron bath

Sierra wall furniture by G PLAN
E. Gomme Limited, High Wycombe, Buckinghamshire

ornamented with griffon's feet and acanthus leaves, while Porcelain Jungle installed a neo-classical bidet. 'Colour', says Sally, 'unifies everything. Colour and texture.' They calculate they must have tried over seventy different shades of paint before finding the correct 'cramoisy', supplied by DemiGod Paints of Ilchester. This lends the whole house a satisfying blush, softened by the addition of authentic nineteenth-century lime and horsehair to the mix. 'The lime and horsehair humanize it', Peter declares. 'Without them, the walls would be merely . . . *flat*.'

. . . And there are the themes. One shape: a simple semi-pointed arch. (Fox: 'I see it as Mughal. You could call it Gothic, but it isn't.') Three colours: saturated powder blue, sedate grey and matt white . . . There are sub-plots, and secondary games with pink, green and lilac, but the dominant themes are like handholds in this fell-bordering farmhouse . . . Keith explains: 'Fox, you must understand, has the taste. She's out in front. But sometimes I push in front to balance her lightness, dreaminess. More *weight*, I say, there must be more weight . . .'

The World of Interiors,
February 1985

'After lengthy consultation with a heating engineer now in Matteawan, my wife and I installed a pipeless furnace inlaid with emeralds and jade which feeds the warmth directly into an upstairs clothes closet, leaving the rest of the establishment at freezing point. This ingenious arrangement has two advantages: it scents the house with an acrid, invigorating smell of frying cloth recalling a tailor shop in the Bronx, and it permits me to tend two kerosene burners, a Franklin stove, and a fireplace. The children have grown to accept the sooty-faced character with the icicle depending from his nose and the large drum of oil as some weird kind of minstrel, and it's probably just as well.'

S. J. Perelman, *Acres and Pains*

Against this roseate background, Peter and Sally's wonderfully eclectic mix of furnishings hums with vibrant life. An emerald green leather footstool stands demurely by the fire; a fakir's brass sideboard from northern India gleams dimly against a wall; two porcelain skunks chase one another across the landing; a unique collapsible divan-cum-four-seater sofa edged in cadmium velvet welcomes you to the front room; a vast oil portrait of a nineteenth-century munitions tycoon, casts a genial glow over the hall.

Outside, Damian ffrench-Farce turned his attention to the back

garden. 'There used to be a diseased apple tree and a moribund honeysuckle just there', says Sally, gesturing towards a miniature pagoda peeping over a wall of bamboo. 'Damian knew right away that it had to be Japan or nothing. He designed the sand garden, the pagoda, the Shinto temple, the ancestral cemetery, the calligraphy court and the bridge over the lotus pond. All in a space fifteen feet by twelve. It's a masterpiece of compression.'

The only thing left to be sorted out after eighteen months of hard labour was the disastrous lean-to at the rear of the house. With the aid of another architect friend, a metallurgist and a professor of mechanical engineering from Bristol University, and

assistance from the research and development department of *Aerospatiale*, they designed a steel and glass conservatory in the style of the period, but with many modern and labour-saving features, such as a reversible entrance, hermetically-sealed casements, low-voltage common-earth infra-red lighting and a sprinkler system that runs entirely on shredded copies of *Harpers & Queen*. In it, Sally tends her collection of rare *Cucurbitae oviferae* and *Lycopersica esculentia*, whose flowers fill the air with a delightful scent.

Only one major problem arose during the course of this extensive but meticulously planned renovation exercise. Sally confesses: 'We realized, after we'd had the dividing wall rebuilt between the front room and the back parlour, that it was impossible to get in or out of the back parlour, since we'd also had the doorway closed off and made into a display case for the tortoiseshell medical implements Peter collects. So we thought we would have to lose either the display case or the rebuilt wall – and then an

old friend of ours, who happens to be the Emeritus Professor of Suburban Buildings at the University of Lutterworth, visiting one day, told us that these houses *never actually had a dividing wall between the front room and the back parlour* – so we had to take the whole wall out and remodel the opening in the original style, with a simple lintel and unadorned verticals, which we bought at auction in Fyfe.'

Sally and Peter Herbert are perfectionists – and it shows. Having lavished so much time, money and effort on their house, you might expect it to be a work of art – which, as Peter modestly admits, 'It is.'

YOUR HAIRSTYLE AND MAKE-UP ARE ENTIRELY OUT OF PERIOD, SHARON

Food

When did we get interested in food? What prompted it? Was it when we got our first important jobs and started the expense-account lunch routine? Was it when we started to feel just a little grown-up, and asked people Round To Dinner? Was it when we started dating our Our Wife/Husband and concluded that a bag of chips and a spring roll was probably short of the mark for romance? Was it simply a need to grow out of our teens and twenties, when we scarfed up indiscriminate and loathsome messes at all hours of the day and night?

Something happened. We became conscious of food. Drink, too. Boys became men when they learnt the difference between a *Médoc* and a *Côte de Nuits* (different shaped bottle); and women became women of the world when they found out that, when in doubt, AC *Sauvignon* and *Chardonnay* were the wines they liked to drink.

And of course, we spend half our lives in each others' houses, eating. Once you get asked round to dinner, you have to ask back. You have to get out the cook books and the fancy attachments for the food processor. And before long, you end up gawping at

. . . The day before, prepare the pears. Peel, halve and core them and place them in a saucepan . . . cover with the wine and a broken cinnamon stick and heat until barely simmering . . . wash the monkfish and pat dry with kitchen paper . . . just as the liquid begins to caramelise, add the lemon juice and stir vigorously . . . reduced to a quarter of its original volume . . . add the cubes one at a time . . . thread the piece of monkfish . . . reserving the liquid . . . baste the fruit continuously . . . intersperse with the pears . . . hand the sauce separately . . .

How to boil an egg:

'*Method 1*. Bring sufficient water to cover the eggs to boil. Gently place the eggs in the water, set the egg-timer or make a note of the time, and cook from 3–4½ min., according to taste. Take out the eggs, tap each lightly, once, with the back of a spoon, and serve.

Method 2. Put the eggs into a pan containing cold water and bring to the boil. When boiling point is reached, start timing. Cooking will take a little less time than with Method 1.'

Mrs. Beeton's Family Cookery

It doesn't have to be this way. But, somehow, it always is.

TWO DINNER PARTIES

They would begin with *Thyme-scented steamed chicken breast with four vegetables* and drink *Hermitage Blanc Le Chevalier de Sterimberg*; there was home-made mango ice-cream garnished with slices of kumquat to follow. It took Paul five hours to buy all the materials from Waitrose, Safeway and a man in the high street with a shop that shut at two-thirty on Saturdays.

Total cost of ingredients, including wine: £63.98

He then spent another three hours combining the ingredients in his kitchen while his wife Kate dressed the dining table and got the children to bed. When the recipe called for a sprig of 'bruised thyme' it added a further twenty minutes while he and Kate deliberated as to whether bruised was the same as battered with a knife handle, or meant merely rubbed between the forefinger and thumb.

Their guests, Michael and Helen, took an hour and forty minutes to eat the repast, which began with *pasta* dressed in sour cream and lumpfish roe and incorporated mature Tilseter cheese (before the pudding) and a selection of hand-crafted miniature biscuits (with the coffee) bought from the Viennese coffee-house on the other side of the railway bridge.

That was the fourth time they'd had Michael and Helen to dinner.

'The standard text of Classical gastronomic literature is Trimalchio's feast from *The Satyricon* of Petronius, a fictional extravaganza built on an unmistakable and amusing basis of fact, during which guests were offered a hare tricked out with wings to look like a Pegasus, a wild sow with its belly full of live thrushes, quinces stuck with thorns to look like sea urchins, a hog stuffed with sausage links, roast pork carved into model fish, and several other frivolities of the kind.'

Reay Tannahill, *Food In History*

I SHALL COOK THEM SOMETHING THOROUGHLY INTIMIDATING.

But that night, all four of them had the same dream . . .

*   *   *

Kate, his wife, put the kids to bed, dressed the dining table and slipped a fresh tape of *The Dam Busters' March* into the stereo. Their guests, Michael and Helen, arrived to a quick *apéritif* of *Malibu* and cheese footballs. By this time, the starter was on the table, and the next course was in the oven.

First came a bowl of Heinz Spaghetti in tomato sauce, accompanied by a Jereboam of *Lutomer Riesling*. Paul had had some difficulty in prising the really caked bits of spaghetti off the bottom of the pan but, with a light wristy action perfected on Wall's sausages which burst their skin, he managed to get all but the blackest fragments out.

Another Methusalah of *Lutomer Riesling* later, it was on to the Safeway own-brand cod fish fingers served on a bed of baked beans, accompanied by large dishes of McCain's oven chips and Findus frozen peas, with a choice of HP sauce or plain ketchup.

For afters, no stone was left unturned: Wall's *Viennetta* vied with two flavours of Bird's Instant Whip for the affections of the eaters, while scattered tantalizingly around the periphery of the table stood bowls of orange-flavoured Matchmakers and a couple of full bottles of *Bailey's Irish Cream*. It took Paul, Kate, Helen and Michael about half an hour to wolf down the lot.

**Total cost of ingredients,
including grog: £57.87.**

That was the fourth time they'd had Helen and Michael to dinner.

BAD FOOD

So what happened to all the muck we grew up with? It's still there, isn't it?

Q: Cast your mind back: what built that young body of yours?

A: Sherbet spaceships, fish fingers, Crunchies, white bread, Munchmallows, Tizer, strawberry Mivvis, Milky Bars, baked beans, Rolos, Wall's ice-cream, Sun-Pat peanut butter, jelly cubes, Coca-Cola, Instant Whip, tinned spaghetti, frozen beefburgers, Liquorice Allsorts, crisps (with the blue twist of salt), Spangles, jam, Battenburg cake, Quality Street, chips, Cidrax, hot-chocolate-drinking-chocolate, frozen peas, fudge, lemon barley water, tinned mushroom soup, Opal Fruits, Rice Crispies, Bisto, steamed syrup sponge and custard.

Q: What goes into, say, a chocolate flavour Bird's Angel Delight?

A: Sugar, Modified Starch, Vegetable Oil (Hydrogenated), Emulsifiers (Propylene Glycol Monostearate, Lecithin), Fat-reduced Cocoa, Gelling Agents (Disodium Monophosphate, Sodium Pyrophosphate), Caseinate, Lactose, Caramel, Whey Powder, Flavourings.

Q: Does any of this have any nutritional value?

A: No.

Q: What should you avoid reading if you like to eat junk?

A: *Pure, White And Deadly*, by Professor John Yudkin. Yudkin is a campaigner against processed sugar, the sort used in massive quantities in many processed foods. Some of his experiments suggested that high levels of processed sugar could lead to coronary thrombosis, diabetes and heart disease.

Q: If we grew up eating so much terrible food, why aren't we all ill?

A: We may well be. Scientists have recently found fat deposits in the arteries of children aged eight.

Health

UNFITNESS

For the first time, things aren't working quite as well as they used to. The temple of the body needs an occasional repair. Bits drop off. The innards are no longer quite as reliable as before (how like the old car parked outside, eh? How fine everything was in that first careless year).

The surface has obviously changed a bit, but keeping track of the insides is harder. And like the muffled grinding of some small, expensive part of your motor which announces unhappiness in the bearings, your body can only make its inner unease known by strange and not easily intelligible signs.

But there it is: to go with your dicky back, grey hairs, paunch, crow's-feet and dewlap, you now have

* late-developer hay fever
* gout (for the hard drinkers)
* runaway baldness
* shortness of breath
* migraines
* carious teeth
* bronchitis in the winter
* recurrent bowel disorders
* stiffness
* memory loss

If not all, then at least some of them. Moreover, you're now at that age when you have to Go Into Hospital in a way which was unthinkable ten years back. Then, hospitalization was a disaster, a tragedy, a cutting-short of your

young life, a hideous sign. Now, it happens pretty much round the clock. Obviously, you go into hospital to have kids – a wonderful thing, by and large. But you also go in, these days, for running repairs.

Sometimes you have your guts investigated after working too hard for too long, and discovering that things have gone astray Down There. Sometimes you have your varicose veins whipped out, or your non-threatening lumps. Sometimes you have wisdom teeth that have hung on in there for so long they won't come out and just lounge about on the X-rays, flicking V-signs. Sometimes you get signs and portents which the quacks can't fathom, but which go down like markers for middle-age. You can't rely on yourself any more.

As you become more and more aware of these little imperfections, you take a look at the kind of life you're living. Could it be (you ask yourself) your diet?

So of course you rifle the fridge and the larder for signs of malpractice, and even though you're a wholemeal bread fan (do you make a fuss over it at hotels in the morning?) and you try to keep up a regime of healthy, dull, fresh fruit eating, the evidence is all there: tinned baked beans; deep frozen specialist pork sausages; stilton. You've reached the stage where, if you're a man, your waist measurement (in inches) is the same as your age (in years).

Time to get things under control.

Stress: A study done by Thomas Holmes and Richard Rahe in 1967 identified stress-provoking times, which Holmes and Rahe called Life Events. A sample of Life Events reveals the following:

Life Event	Stress Score
Death of Partner	100
Divorce	73
Prison Sentence	63
Pregnancy	40
More rows with partner	35
Trouble with in-laws	29
Child starting/ leaving school	26
Change in church-going	19
Change in eating habits	15
Holiday	13
Christmas	12

FITNESS

Three approaches, here: (**1**) go on a diet (**2**) take some exercise (**3**) fanny about with some interesting and expensive alternatives.

(**1**) Have you ever tried to diet? Can you imagine anything more depressing? And why are diet books so humiliating and insulting to read? Remember this, from *The Complete Scarsdale Medical Diet*? ▶

Face the Winter
RADIANTLY
HEALTHY & FIT

WITH perfect inner health you can face Winter cheerfully, really fit. How can you get this inner health? Take Bile Beans regularly.

Purely vegetable Bile Beans, favourite family laxative, help you to cast aside sluggishness, liver and digestive upsets and other minor ills due to constipation. You will feel it's good to be alive whatever the weather.

For fitness, and energy, for keeping youthfully slim and attractive, you need Bile Beans— just a couple at bedtime.

Nature's Gentle Aid
BILE BEANS

WHY YOU WILL SUCCEED NOW REGARDLESS OF PAST FAILURES

The unique, exclusive advantages of the Two-On-One-Off combination plan, and its original elements, make all the difference between past failure and future success for many.

During the first two weeks on the Scarsdale Medical Diet, you will be delighted and *encouraged* by rapid weight loss, actually seeing on the scale that pounds are dropping off day by day (not that discouraging pound or two a week).

Furthermore, although you are losing weight without hunger, feeling better and enjoying increased energy and vigour, you look forward to more food freedom at the end of the fourteen days . . .

One of my patients said to me recently about the Scarsdale Two-On-One-Off combination, 'Dr Tarnower, this is the ultimate lifetime program. I may have other problems one of these days, but overweight is never again going to be one of them' . . .

What level of credulity do you need to swallow all that? And yet this is the kind of thing that made a fortune for Dr Tarnower and is, in its way, replicated in all diet books: this mixture of ruthlessness, optimism and fatuity. And then you pick up something a bit more up-to-the-minute, such as Geoffrey Cannon and Hetty Einzig's *Dieting Makes You Fat*, and you read this:

For a sedentary person a lifetime spent between diets is not only self-defeating but dangerous. Every diet trains the body to adapt to dieting, which it does by slowing itself down, losing some lean tissue and not replacing all of it . . .

Dieting makes you fat because of this cumulative change in the composition of the body. A second reason why dieting makes you fat is that fat is lighter than muscle . . . A third reason why dieting makes you fat is because fat is less metabolically active than muscle . . . the one sure way to slow the body down and so create the conditions for getting fat is to go on a diet . . . Habitual dieters are on a downward spiral which remorselessly reduces their vitality . . .

Tough, eh? So you don't go on a diet, exactly: you merely acquire a consciousness (or a conscience)

about what you're eating. You feel guilty when you scoff a sherry trifle; you feel virtuous when you grill a piece of white fish. You nag yourself. And then you try

(2) Exercise. This really denotes the passing of time. In your twenties, you took as much exercise as a woodworm. Who cared? You were thin, you stayed thin. You stayed up all night, you ate, you drank, you stayed thin and you had oceans of energy. Then you turned thirty, started to nod off at ten-thirty and had attacks of the Blue Spots when you ran up a flight of stairs. So you bought some jogging shoes. You actually did it. You bought some bloody jogging shoes (not just

Tests reveal that sickness can result from excessive adherence to many physical fitness regimes.

Every pair of training shoes should carry a government health warning: 'Danger: jogging can damage your health' . . .

Norfolk goes on to point out that people who go jogging in the city for half an hour can absorb the equivalent of 10 to 20 cigarettes' worth of carbon monoxide ('Jogging is completely unnecessary,' according to cardiologist George Sheenan, who wrote one of the early jogging handbooks, *Running And Being*. 'A good brisk walk is equivalent to a jog any time'); that when a lightly-built eight-stone person runs around on a hard surface, his/her knees suffer a momentary weight equivalent to three-quarters of a ton with each step he/she takes; that dieting and exercises together can cause hormonal imbalances, infertility and period loss in women; that the death rate of stressed, worried, prejudiced-against-smoking non-smokers can be three times as high as that of relaxed smokers. And that, basically, people who worry about being well and fit and healthy and so on are prone to dieting, exercising and worrying themselves sick.

A recent article by Donald Norfolk (author of *Think Well, Feel Great*) said, among other things

jogging shoes, with air-suspension heels, but shorts, two T-shirts, two pairs of running socks, a sweatshirt, a book on dieting and exercise, and a rowing machine/fitness centre for wet days costing £117.85).

Or perhaps you started to work out in the gym round the corner from the office. Or you joined a sports club. You signed up for tennis lessons (out comes the shorty tennis skirt, a volley of wolf-whistles from the labourers outside, and off to the courts where the horrid male instructor drills you as if you're in the Green Berets). You looked up the late opening times of the local pool but never got round to going.

You did all these things. And how do you feel as a consequence? Do you feel, by any chance, awful?

Maybe you try

(3) Massage . . . aromatherapy (being rubbed with significant oils) . . . massive vitamin consumption . . . reflexology (having your feet massaged) . . . the Bach Herbal Remedies (wolfsbane for a cold in the head; samphire for ingrowing toenails, and so on) . . .

The beauty of these is (a) they require very little labour from the person indulging in them: you leave that kind of thing to the toiling masseuse or sinewy aromatherapist (b) they're prettily packaged and attractive to use (c) they often involve other people who can supply your spiritual needs by becoming a confessor to you while you're on the slab/under the thumb/ getting oiled. And they're smart things to do: they cost real money.

Bill Jarman, ninety-year-old former electrician at Bedales School, quizzed on being that old:

Verdict on youth of today: *'I get on with everybody.'*

Changes for the better since his youth: *'Nothing.'*

Things most missed from youth: *'Eyesight. Can no longer see TV.'*

Smoking: *'Twenty Woodbine a day since the age of twelve.'*

Tip for longevity: *'Brisk walks. Be careful when you cross the road.'*

Whatever we do, we consume: advice; time; products. And for many of us, we only really know we're alive when we're consuming.

Music

Musically, some of us begin and end with the Gods of the Sixties: The Beatles (or as it might be, Bob Dylan, or The Beach Boys, or The Who). Others, whose teenage years were spent in the first half of the Seventies, grew up with a corrupt mixture of Sixties heroes (Jimi Hendrix, Simon and Garfunkel, The Rolling Stones, Procul Harum) and Seventies efflorescences (Led Zeppelin, David Bowie, The Carpenters, Elton John, the original Genesis with Peter Gabriel). Others formed their tastes on the other side of the 1976 watershed: this means that the music they grew up with (the most potent music of all) was *Never Mind The Bollocks. Passim.*

We can never give up our favourite music – no matter how awful we secretly understand it to be – because it is too close to us. It very nearly *is* us: as personal and as deeply embedded as childhood memories of Christmas or school terms.

THERE THEY ARE, THE ICONS OF MY TEENAGE REBELLION.

But do we listen to this stuff when we're with other people? No. We listen to:

VAN MORRISON
DIRE STRAITS
FINE YOUNG CANNIBALS
THE CHRISTIANS
B. B. KING
EURYTHMICS
ERIC CLAPTON
PAUL SIMON
THE J. GEILS BAND
TRACEY CHAPMAN

This is the music playing in a thousand thousand houses while we have our drinks and eat our meals and stand up and shout. So there's a division here, between the music of society – this kind of stuff, wallpaper music – and the music we can't admit to.

So what do we do about those pieces of music which are effectively our own property – which are so adolescent or tuneless or rebarbative or just mediocre that we can't justify wasting anyone else's time with them – but which are important to us? When do we listen to them?

We listen to them in the car. We look forward to an hour's drive to an appointment, because it's then that we dust off *American Pie* or *Band On The Run* or *Led Zeppelin II* or *London Calling* and snap it into our car's entertainment system. Soundproofed and travelling at speed, we can enjoy every moment of it, without risking offence or ridicule.

Look at the motorways when they're busy. There you will see thousands of cars speeding by, each with the driver alone, his head thrown back as he yells the words aloud, her fist slapping the wheel in time to the beat, thousands of silent screams hareing up the M1 to get to that meeting on schedule.

Let's make a baby

COUNTDOWN TO CHAOS

'Marriage can succeed for an artist only where there is enough money to save him from taking on uncongenial work and a wife who is intelligent enough to understand and respect the working of the unfriendly cycle of the creative imagination. She will know at what point domestic happiness begins to cloy, where love, tidiness, rent, rates, clothes, entertaining, and rings at the doorbell should stop, and will recognize that there is no more sombre enemy of good art than the pram in the hall.'

Cyril Connolly, *Enemies of Promise*

 Kate and Paul reach a watershed: married for three years, new home with two floors and a small back garden, Kate is *thirty-one*, has become critically aware of the Biological Clock. Paul agonizes. 8 p.m.: Kate throws away her packet of Pills. Evening is consummated with a display of ardour which surprises both parties.

 Kate purchases vastly over-priced pregnancy test kit.

 Kate over-optimistically employs over-priced kit. Result: negative. Back to the drawing-board.

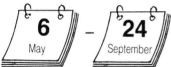 Drawing-board in use.

Getting a bit hacked off, now, but still manage fresh display of ardour. Ardour begins at 11.57 p.m.

Six minutes past midnight: insemination occurs. Male and female nuclei enlarge and move towards the centre of the ovum. There they coalesce to form a single nucleus. That's it. It's there. Paul falls asleep with shattering abruptness.

Kate uses the vastly over-priced pregnancy test kit at 7 a.m., while having a pee. 7.01 a.m.: Kate runs shrieking into bedroom, brandishing the test kit like a Sacred Object. Paul, asleep up to that point, springs vertically from the bed. Satisfaction and horror jostle for position on his face. Kate dances around the room. Paul claps his hand to his head three or four times. No one can understand how it happened so fast.

Kate obtains a copy of Sheila Kitzinger's *The New Good Birth Guide* and Gordon Bourne's *Pregnancy* and starts looking for a hospital that gets two stars and is nearby. There isn't one. Both resolve to wait until the GP has performed the pregnancy test before telling anyone, even though the GP's pregnancy test uses much the same sort of chemistry as the commercial one and is hardly more reliable or definitive.

Paul furtively investigates the section in *Pregnancy* which details the part he played in the business. Gets as far as this: *Migration of Sperms:* 'Approximately 400 million sperms are present in each ejaculation . . . if only 10 per cent of the sperms reach the cervical canal a total of approximately 40 million sperms will have reached this favourable haven. The journey of about 23 centimetres from the cervix, up the uterus and along the Fallopian tubes takes approximately 45 minutes and between 1,000 and 2,000 sperms reach the outer portion of the Fallopian tube . . .' Paul resolves to hide the book.

Bored GP confirms that, yes, Kate is pregnant. Sleepily goes into spiel about what kind of care would she like, has she chosen a hospital yet, how does she feel generally, this is her first, isn't it, a lot of nonsense talked nowadays about

THE DEPTHS

active births and so on, what people fail to realize is that birth is potentially highly dangerous for the mother *and* the child and that with a bit of foresight and the right equipment it's possible to etc., etc., etc. . . . Kate drifts into a deep gloom shortly after leaving the doctor's surgery.

Tell both lots of parents (Paul's mother and father; Kate's mother and step-father and father and step-mother). Paul's M and F overwhelmed and mildly hysterical. Kate's F and S-M extremely pleased. Kate's M and S-F narrowly disapproving. Kate's M in particular gets v. waspish on the subject, assumes that this will be the end of Kate's career, she'll turn into a huge cow and smell of milk.

Tell everyone else.

Kate is sick in the back of a taxi. ('You bloody women. That'll smell for weeks.') Feels sick when she goes near any of the following: pâté, marmalade, petrol, coffee, shellfish, old clothes, Paul's aftershave, the insides of certain cars, pubs, fried bacon, chutney, warm plastic.

Paul pats Kate on the back. She throws up.

Paul gives Kate a kiss. She throws up.

Kate borrows a copy of *What Every Pregnant Woman Should Know*, by Gail Sforza Brewer and Tom Brewer, MD. Reads the following chapter headings:

The Question Doctors Don't Ask
Weight Control: a hazard in pregnancy
Low-Salt Diets: why they don't work
Understanding Swelling

Metabolic Toxemia of Late Pregnancy
'Toxemia' in the Well-Nourished
Other Pregnancy Complications
The Afflicted Child
'What Medical School Did You Graduate From?' – The
Doctor's Training Excludes Nutrition

Decides to hide copy of *What Every Pregnant Woman Should Know.*

6
December

Kate and Paul choose a hospital. Built circa 1880, bits drop off the outside and have to be caught in a wire net hung over the door. Inside, it looks as if it's been used for tank practice. A smell of bodies and old food, weakly masked by chemicals, hangs over everything. A terrific midwife hales them up and down stairs to the first antenatal session. Paul makes a mental note to skip the other appointments. A consultant with fly-away silver hair and an offensively breezy manner asks Kate to pop up on the table and just pop her pants down. He goes on to talk about (a) fly-fishing (b) car repair bills (c) rugger, with Paul while his hand is up Kate. Kate, in deep depression, seeks solace in *The New Good Birth Guide.* Reads the following:

. . . Obstetricians, too, have been shocked when women asked not to have an enema. A woman told me recently that when she said that she would prefer not to have one, her obstetrician exclaimed: 'Not have an enema? There will be shit on the walls, shit in me boots, shit everywhere!'

Resolves to hide book.

Paul gets deeply drunk at a New Year's Eve party, where those friends who already have children get wheezily maudlin and dilate on the sheer *cost* of small kids versus the sheer *joy* of small kids; while those who don't have kids elbow him constantly, calling him a bit of a sharp-shooter, a devil, a sperm-bank, a prong, a peopler of nations and an irresponsible git.

> Gallup ran a survey of 400 parents with babies aged 18 months or less. Some had worked out that their tiny ones were costing them over £200 a month. That's £2,500 a year. At least. After tax. The loot went on nannies, childminders, nappies, clothes, food and toys, with the nappies alone costing more than £300 a year.

Parcel arrives from Paul's mother. It contains two enormous hand-knitted cardigans big enough for an orang-utan, and a pair of woollen tights that Pavarotti could have worn. This marks the onset of the layette season.

Nothing happens. Nothing except swellings, ripenings, kicks and bumps. A scan at the hospital reveals something looking like a mango seen through the wrong end of a very dirty telescope in a thick fog with rain approaching. Everyone is enormously excited and Kate and Paul keep the Polaroid snap of the Mango. More bits of layette arrive from all parties, including a romper-suit with a picture of Horace the Happy Horse on it, which Paul furtively throws in the dustbin. Auntie who appears to belong to neither Paul nor Kate's family sends a pair of wool bootees too small to fit anything except a couple of radishes. Kate starts antenatal classes. A puny midwife fumbles with exploding plaster wombs, plastic foetuses, rubber birth canals and disentegrating umbilical cords. Everyone goes into deep breathing exercises at the end with the lights turned off. Colossal farting poisons the air.

2 May

Two months to go. Paul and Kate panic. They buy a cot, a changing table, a convertible buggy/pram, a baby seat to go in the back of the car, a changing mat, a night-light, a sterilizing unit, five large bottles plus teats, five small bottles plus teats, five baby-grows (newborn size), three undervests (newborn size), three pairs of socks (newborn size), a mobile with four fluffy ducks dancing around a clockwork mechanism that plays the *Brahms Lullaby*, a wallpaper frieze with chickens on it which Paul has to put up in the nursery, a van-sized packet of newborn nappies, a tub of cream to put on the kid's bottom, a bucket of white emulsion to freshen up the nursery walls, a lampshade with more chickens on it to brighten up the nursery light, a parasol to go on the buggy and a breast pump for expressing milk.

4 May

Think about names. Purchase copy of *The Modern Book of Babies' Names*, by Hilary Spence. Book seems to contain only the following:

Boys' names:

Fabron (French, *'The little blacksmith'*)

Knut (Norse, *'The knot'*)

Toft (Anglo-Saxon, *'A small farm'*)

Bowie (Gaelic, *'Yellow haired'*)

Este (Italian, *'Man from the East'*)

Laidley (Anglo-Saxon, *'From the water-meadow'*)

Ruff (French, *'The red haired one'*)

Frick (Anglo-Saxon, *'Bold man'*)

Girls' names:

Helice (Greek, *'Spiral'*)

Quenby (Scandinavian, *'Womanly'*)

Zona (Latin, *'A girdle'*)

Cyrilla (Latin, *'Lordly one'*)

Storm (Anglo-Saxon, *'A tempest'*)

Bevin (Gaelic, *'Melodious Lady'*)

Ora (Latin, *'The she-bear'*)

Fritzi (Teutonic, *'Peaceful ruler'*)

27 May

Braxton Hicks contraction? Paul flies into spasm of terror. Kate is curiously relaxed.

5 June

Name for girl: Rebecca.

7 June

Another Braxton Hicks. Paul tears round the room, looking for the hospital's number. By the time he's found it, the emergency has long gone.

12 June

Name for boy: Tom. Wouldn't you know it.

14 June

Paul goes to men's antenatal class. There he's shown a video of a birth, plus still colour pictures, plus the exploding models and the collapsing rubberware. He learns about episiotomies, afterbirth, breech births, gas and air, pushing, breathing, lifting, shoving, bearing down, crapping, shouting and swearing, blood, pulsing umbilici, apgar tests and Vivaldi tapes (for relaxation in labour). He congratulates himself on not fainting or throwing up at any of this and drinks heavily for the rest of the evening.

We are now entering the danger zone. The baby may or may not be due at any time. Braxton Hicks contractions zing around. Kate looks like a parked camper-caravan, grumbles about the weight. Paul can hardly get near her. The bump keeps kicking and punching through the night.

Right. The baby's overdue. Arguably. Well, when are we counting from? Well, when was your last period? Well, what's the doctor written in the book? My God this last nine months has gone quickly, *my God*, the thing'll be *here* before you know it. Don't call it the *thing*.

2.16 a.m. Kate wakes Paul up. The contractions! MY GOD! THE CONTRACTIONS! Kate plods up and down the bedroom, gasping and complaining. What is it? One contraction every forty minutes? No! Contractions lasting forty seconds? How far apart? TIME THEM!! Every, what, four minutes? Going down . . . three and a half . . . are you sure? AM I SURE??? The car, the car, the hospital bag (it's all packed, where the hell is it?) call the hospital, hello, my wife's having a baby, who am I talking to? Well, she's walking around, shouting, I would say she was having a baby, shall I bring her in, I'm sorry, I dropped the phone, bring her in, right, I'll bring her in. Right. *CAR*. Where have I left the CAR? It's OUTSIDE, you left it there specially. Through the middle-of-the-night streets, seem to have forgotten how to drive, is this the gear lever? Should I fill up with petrol just in case? Is this the hospital? Seems to have changed. Resembles cross between church and prison at this hour. GET IN. Into the delivery room. WHOOSH. *It's actually happening.* Five centimetres dilated? Is that good or bad? Do you want gas and air? How would you like me to be supportive? DON'T TOUCH ME YOU IDIOT. No. Of course. (Shouting and swearing, here, as predicted.) I AM NOT FUCKING SHOUTING AND SWEARING. And so on and so on for another hour and a half, sweating and dazed, until at 4.48 a.m., extremely painfully, out comes young Tom (not such a bad name; commonplace, I know), emerging head looking like a terrifically cross blue Brussels sprout, splosh go the fluids, splat goes the placenta and *there he is*. My God. Another person. World person number 6 billion and 1. What a little beauty he is.

Working mothers get a bad deal in this country. According to one piece of research (*Managing Mothers*, by Julia Brannen and Peter Moss) working mothers not only do most of the household chores when they get back from work, they actually expect to do so. One woman said (despite having a nanny for her two kids): 'I do the washing one night, the ironing another. Monday and Tuesday I don't do anything except correspondence. I look after all the bills and accounts. My husband does not do anything.'

Ten things you should know about your nanny

1 Nannies come from an ad in the back of *The Lady*, and are *cordon bleu* chefs in their spare time.
2 Daily nannies live approximately 150 miles from your house, and have to leave home at 3 a.m. to get to you by 9. This is something which they manage on the first day, and then never repeat.
3 Nannies consume twice their own body weight in low-fat fruit yoghurt every week.
4 Nannies re-tune every radio in the house to Radio 1.
5 You must never let the nanny make your bed. Close to, it's as foully revelatory as a secret diary.
6 Nannies never have boyfriends who are articled accountants or trainee solicitors. Nannies' boyfriends are squaddies, garage mechanics, heavy metal guitarists, students of textile design, assistants at the cold meat counter of the nearest supermarket, Christian evangelists.
7 Nannies consider it an essential part of their job to buy hundreds and hundreds of scented nappy disposal sacks. These remain unused for the entire time that the child is in nappies. Then they are thrown away.
8 A nanny who is unhappy with her work will never tell you outright. Instead, she will let her feelings be known by (a) putting your best white shirt in the wash with a leaky indigo sweater, or (b) almost *but not quite* removing baby puke from the sitting-room carpet.
9 A happy nanny gets into fist-fights with the children.
10 All nannies come from Yorkshire or Surrey.

Married sex

> 'There is a misapprehension that women describing sex is attractive. It isn't. The best-selling sexually explicit blockbuster phenomenon is to do with money, nothing to do with literature. I long for a blockbuster that's also good writing.'
>
> Anita Brookner, interviewed by Val Hennessy, *A Little Light Friction*

From *Quantity Surveyor!*, Joeleen Clinch's latest torrid outpouring:

• • •

Maxwell Wolveridge stirred uneasily between the sheets of his king-sized Sleepeezee. The dawn light filtered through the half-closed curtains. His eyes opened.

Leatherhead.

The name echoed for a second in his mind.

Leatherhead!

At once Maxwell was up, yawning, stretching his tall, un-tanned body in the chilly air. He looked over to where Claudettina was lying, still asleep. Even at that hour of the day, he couldn't help admiring her voluptuous curves, her tousled gravy-brown hair, her nightie.

What a night *that* had been! He couldn't take too many more like that . . .

And besides, Leatherhead was waiting. He had a major gig to prepare for – on-site inspection at the new Safeway development. God alone knew what the traffic would be like on the freeway, through the mean streets of Edgware, down to the inferno that was the A406, on through gloomy Tolworth and Chessington, out to the no-man's-land that was Leatherhead. Leatherhead: where only the young are free.

He looked down. Peering over the rim of his paunch, he

could see a hard-on. He looked back at Claudettina. Was this the time?

'You off?' she mumbled sleepily.

No. Maybe this wasn't the time.

•   •   •

Claudettina watched Zitney Trench as he went through the routine: the hand running through the hair, the deepening bark of his voice, the purposeful flexing of his shoulders. What a per-former this guy was. One of the best.

'And if they're not in by tomorrow morning – and I *mean* tomorrow morning – you can assume that we'll be buying our photocopying paper *elsewhere!*'

Zitney slammed down the phone. He looked up.

'Goddamned pen-pushers', he snarled. 'Don't know if they're having a shit or a shave.'

'You wanted this, Zitney.' Claudettina placed the report on his desk.

'Yeah. Thanks, baby.'

MATRIMONIAL-HARMONICS.

Zitney's brow furrowed. She watched him as he read the report. Her eyes travelled across his broad shoulders, his hard, tanned face, and his dark, swept-back hair. Zitney looked up again.

'Great. Could you take it to Swindon Blowfeather for initialling? I, er, I need to be away from the office this afternoon.'

Claudettina raised an eyebrow.

'Do you need me to come with you?'

Almost before the words had left her mouth, she felt a stab of excitement. *For God's sake! She was a married woman* – and here she was, offering her body to Zitney Trench like some foxy bitch with the craziest passion on the brain and superheated sex between the legs. Zitney fixed her with the kind of look that made her feel electric all over.

'It's okay. It's only an appointment with my dental hygienist.'

TWO WOMEN WHO HAD AFFAIRS:

'I dressed for sex and thought about nothing else on these trips to London and, once I was locked away with Andrew, I got up to all sorts of things I would have been too embarrassed to do with Tony. And *that* was what was so exciting.'

While a woman whose husband had an affair said:

'The morning after he admitted that he was in love with another woman, I lay on our bed as if suspended in space. Downstairs I heard my husband quietly exchanging words in a telephone call to his mistress. A few minutes later he appeared and said he must go to her. Poor love, he said, she was so upset.'

'Really, it was a game in which I made the rules: always being the one to decide whether or not we'd make love when we met. I don't think I have ever before felt quite so much in control and it's really a powerful sensation . . .'

'Get a load of *her* . . .' Milton Humberside's eyes narrowed as he sipped his lethal cocktail of Foster's lager and concentrated lime juice – a drink for gamblers, heartbreakers, hell-raisers. A drink for The Joker in the Pack.

Maxwell nodded as they watched a little, hustling minx sashay her way across the floor. She was pert, nubile and willing. Her breasts jutted against the thick fabric of her duffle coat. Milton took another sip of his cocktail.

'Jeez, I could do with some leg-over', he sighed, settling back in his seat. 'I mean, I love my wife, but . . . there has to be *more*, right? There has to be more than *Newsnight* . . .'

Maxwell watched him closely. Was this the Milton Humberside he'd known so long? The Milton Humberside who'd clawed his way to the middle of the heating and lighting installation business in the space of only ten years? The Milton Humberside whose looks could make a woman turn weak at the knees, and whose ducted fluorescent shelf units were in use from Hartlepool to Exeter and back again? The Milton Humberside, dammit, who used to Do It *all night long*?

'What's up, Milt?'

'Ah, I dunno. Just – how old are you, Max?'

'Thirty-three.'

'Thirty-three. Right. You got kids?'

'One. Girl.'

'Yeah? I got three.'

'Three?' Milton Humberside had three kids? The news shook Maxwell Wolveridge like a hammer-blow. *Three kids . . . no wonder.*

'Exactly. I get home. I read them a story – not the baby, of course – I go downstairs, I eat, I turn on the news . . . I wake up, it's half-past midnight, Davina's gone to bed – the kid wakes up at five every morning, little bastard – and then I fall asleep again. I mean . . .'

Maxwell looked at him. His hard, lopsidedly handsome face was tense.

'What's it all about, this marriage game, anyway?'

Maxwell stared long and hard into his small Guinness. Faces from the past seemed to come back and taunt him – Carmina Twist, the gypsy-eyed temptress from his university days; Vauxhall Nova, his first great love, the woman who'd taught him to say 'When'; Lal Basingstoke – big, blonde, beautiful, inexhaustible, extremely tiring Lal Basingstoke. All these women. And now?

'It's a bit of a business.'

'Absolutely. I say, look at *her*.'

In a recent MORI survey, only 52 per cent of those questioned thought that having sexual relations with someone who is married to someone else was morally wrong. This put it some way below soccer hooliganism, which 75 per cent thought was wrong, and the use of soft drugs such as cannabis (60 per cent).

That night, Maxwell reached across the Sleepeezee to where Claudettina lay. He ran his hand down her shoulder blade. She stirred, turning to face him. They kissed. Her hand snaked down his pyjamas to feel his hardness . . .

Then it was morning. Dammit! They'd fallen asleep again!

● ● ●

I AM NOT SLEEPING WITH SOMEONE ELSE. AS A MATTER OF FACT, WE STAY AWAKE.

Claudettina was a woman. And Zitney was a man. And that was all that mattered as they cruised down the freeway, alone together in Zitney's gleaming red hatchback.

'Godammit,' muttered Zitney, looking out through the windscreen, 'I musta missed the turn.'

'I don't think so', Claudettina replied, languorously. 'And anyway, what's it to you? You don't give a damn about whether we get back in time for the meeting.'

'Don't I?' Zitney's eyes narrowed. 'It should say A404 somewhere along here . . .'

'After all, we've been to Charteris's house. We've been through his tax arrangements. We've got the cheque. What's the rush?'

Zitney slowed the car into the left-hand lane. He snatched a quick glance at her. Maybe she was right. What was the rush? Wasn't it fine just to cruise the freeway, in the afternoon sunshine, a foxy lady in the seat beside you . . .

No. There was no chance. No way. No way he, Zitney Trench could tell her, Claudettina Wolveridge, née Schlitz, the way he felt when she half-closed her eyes at him, or reached up to take a boxfile down from the section marked 'Insolvency'. This wasn't what it was all about. *This wasn't what you did on a Tuesday afternoon.* Claudettina stretched in her seat. Her hand brushed his, resting on the gear lever. 'Mm. You have got hairy hands', she said.

He looked down. They were kind of hairy.

'Are you hairy all over?'

What was she *saying*, she thought to herself. *What the hell are you doing?* You crazy slut! If only Maxwell could be more . . . if only they could stay awake . . . if only Maxwell could be with her at three thirty in the afternoon, when they might do it like the old days . . .

'Yes, I am kind of hairy.' Zitney's voice broke the uncomfortable silence. Thank God, he thought. I don't have a hard-on. Too damn tired. Thank God.

● ● ●

Quinine Trench, Zitney's wife of twelve years, lay in bed, flicking slowly through a Jackie Collins. Zitney lay beside her, his firm, lean shoulder in the air, the sheet tangled negligently around his bronzed arm. His rough snores broke the stillness. She caressed his back. He went on snoring. And what a snore he had . . . strong, long, thick and hard, it was a snore that went on all night long, a snore that *never* let up, baby! . . . a snore that reached the highest heights and the deepest depths, a snore that took you up among the stars and down into the very inside of yourself. Maybe that was why she'd married him, all those years ago. That was the kind of woman she was. And that, it turned out, was the kind of man he was.

She squeezed his ass. Unconscious, he flicked her hand away and coughed.

She went back to her Jackie Collins, untouched.

And that was how she liked it.

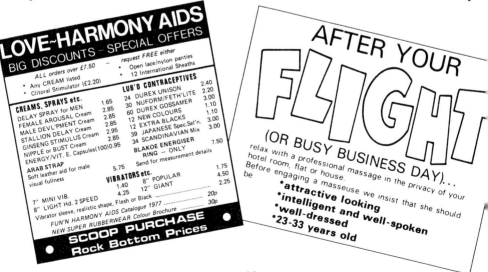

Schools

1 EXT. AN EDWARDIAN BUILDING. DAY.

RICHARD and EMMA are standing at the front door of a rambling, untidy, Edwardian mansion. It is, in fact, CLUMBER PARK Preparatory School, for boys and girls to the age of 13.

The first true prep schools were started in the nineteenth century, in the confused wake of the great public schools. Names such as Lambrook, Stubbington House, Orwell Park and Hawtreys date from this time. As the state system sinks slowly beneath the waves, the old prep schools become more and more desirable for middle-class parents (especially London middle-class parents) to send their kids to.

RICHARD is in his mid-thirties, wearing a collar and tie and a blazer. EMMA is about the same age, dressed in a longish navy skirt and low-heeled courts. They both look apprehensive.

EMMA (*an edge in her voice*)	Why don't you try it again?
RICHARD (*likewise*)	I just have.

91

2   INT. THE ENTRANCE HALL OF THE SCHOOL. DAY.

Inside, there are notice boards nailed to the panelling, with details of school outings, charity events, term activities. One board is covered with photographs of a trip to Waddesdon Manor in the School Bus. A fine layer of dust rests on everything. A distant cry can be heard issuing from a classroom.

MR BACON strides across the lino'd floor to the front door. He's in his late forties, tall, has a good deal of rather wild, greying hair, and a cardigan that must have been home-made.

3   EXT. THE FRONT DOOR OF THE SCHOOL. DAY.

EMMA and RICHARD, as before, busy in debate:

RICHARD   Maybe he's deaf . . .
EMMA   I've forgotten his name . . .
(suddenly panicky)

On which the door swings open to reveal MR BACON, his eyes bulging slightly, his hair wafting in the draught. He smiles grimly at them.

MR BACON   Yes?

4   INT. THE MAIN HALL OF THE SCHOOL. DAY.

MR BACON is into his grand tour of the school. EMMA and RICHARD shuffle along anxiously in his wake, trying to take it in.

MR BACON   For *me*, a school is more than a place where the children
(gesturing   learn their ABC and their times-table. For *me*, Clumber Park
around the   has to give *every child* a proper sense of what is *right* and
place)   what is *wrong* . . .

A TEN-YEAR-OLD BOY scuttles past . . .

MR BACON   Alexander!
(rounding on the boy)
BOY   Yes, Mr Bacon.
(a whisper)
MR BACON   *Have we cleaned up in the computer room?*
BOY   Yes, Mr Bacon. All except the bits in the corner.
(inaudible)

WESTMINSTER SCHOOL.

or___Dr Busby settling accounts with Master Billy and his Playmates.

Illustrious Busby, might merit more regard:
Ah! Busby too tender for a stroke so hard " Vide Pollad.

Pub.ᵈ Feb.ᵧ 4ᵗʰ 1785, by J. Ridgeway, Piccadilly

'. . . I have meant to write to you a hundred times during the last three weeks but at all hours of the day I have been busied with teaching and beating and supervising footballings until when at last after all the animals were caged up and I at last had some peace, I have been too sad & too weary to write anything.

You have probably heard that I found it impossible to afford living in London any longer and have come here as a master. It is not really, I suppose, a bad school as schools go but it is a sorry waste of time & energy . . .'

Evelyn Waugh, letter to Harold Acton, February 1925, while Waugh was a teacher at Arnold House prep school in Denbighshire.

5 INT. A CLASSROOM. DAY.

MR BACON has just flung the door open on a room full of eight-year-olds, sitting at their desks. They all wear the same basic uniform. Their TEACHER is a terrified-looking woman in her late twenties.

MR BACON	And *this* – this is where we learn *creative writing* – isn't that so, Miss Cotton?
TEACHER (*braving it out*)	Oh, absolutely.
MR BACON	We had a *local author* here last term. Didn't we, Miss Cotton?
TEACHER	Two local authors, actually . . .
MR BACON	But the second one didn't count. Did he?
TEACHER	He was a bit . . .
MR BACON (*closing the door*)	*Quite.*

6 INT. EMMA & RICHARD'S HOME. NIGHT.

RICHARD is sitting at a table, poring morosely over his cheque-book stubs.

RICHARD (*muttering*)	. . . Clumber Park, thirty pounds . . . St Mostyn's, forty pounds . . . Jesus, forty pounds . . . Gander Hall, twenty-five pounds plus one hundred non-returnable two years before he starts . . . Cake Place, sixty quid . . . *sixty quid* . . .? Bastards . . .

7   EXT. FRONT DOOR OF JANE'S HOUSE. DAY.

EMMA is leaving JANE's nice middle-class house. She stands in the doorway, chatting with JANE. JANE is about six foot two and built to match. She has a red face and a manner that pulls people up short.

> JANE . . . No chance. No chance of getting in. List closed . . . last year . . .
>
> EMMA But he's only *six months old*!
>
> JANE Doesn't matter with St Levin's. Have to put 'em down before they're conceived. True.
>
> EMMA But, I mean, *how* . . .?
>
> JANE *(confidently)* Didn't even bother with Freddie. Didn't even try. Took one look, thought, even if we have a prodigy, never get in. Waste of effort, money. Put him down for five or six places, got in at Gander Hall, loves the place. Stick it out till Common Entrance. Got him down for Harrow after that, and if he doesn't get in, Redfern Park.
>
> EMMA What about State Schools?
>
> JANE What? The one near you? Must be joking. Three years behind St Levin's at the age of eight. Never get anywhere. Two just been expelled for stealing cars. Am I depressing you?

8 INT. EMMA & RICHARD'S HOUSE. DAY.

EMMA and RICHARD are at the breakfast table. TOBY, their six-month-old son, sits in his high chair and is quietly sick. RICHARD is reading a letter.

> RICHARD   . . . Yes . . . he's . . . yes! 'Look forward to welcoming Toby
> (*near hysteria*)   to the reception class in four years' time!' Ha!
> EMMA   Mr Bacon? Fantastic!
> RICHARD   Christ . . . what a relief! What a weight gone! Thank God . . .

A moment's pause. He wipes away a tear. EMMA reaches across the table and squeezes his hand. He looks thoughtfully at TOBY.

> At present rates, an average
> private education will cost you
> about £50,000 by the end.

9 INT. EMMA & RICHARD'S HOUSE. EVENING.

In the living-room. EMMA, RICHARD and MIKE. MIKE is a young-middle-aged guy with a polyester suit and a Samsonite attaché case. This is open, and disgorging papers and leaflets.

> MIKE   See, school fee inflation . . .

He reaches for a booklet and starts to flip through it.

> . . . it's in here, somewhere . . . I mean, it's some astronomical figure, I can't remember what, something terrible like ninety-five per cent . . . anyway, the point is that – oh, here we are. What are we talking about? Ten years from now? Something like that? Well, your average fees per term, ten years on, at current inflation rates . . . will stand at . . . five thousand a term, give or take, you see . . . and that's just when he's ten . . . course it'll be double that by the time he's seventeen . . .

He picks up his pocket calculator. Taps away at it.

> . . . And then there might be another little sibling. I don't know what you've got planned, there, but a decent boys' day school is not something to be entered into lightly, it's a hell of a commitment, I mean I send mine to the local

1   Lacrosse stick (obtainable from school)
1 pr   Black lacrosse boots
1 pr   ~~Brown~~ gym shoes
         white

4 prs   Fawn nylon stockings
                    Hose
                U.IV upwards: 30 denier
                U.III, L.IV : 60 denier
s   Royal blue Wolsey Harlequin
         narrow rib stockings
                   Shoes
         Brown outdoor shoes, lace-up:
         e.g. Clark's 'Runabout'
         Brown indoor shoes: Jun
         strap shoes with re
         lark's 'Rosa
         Nora'

INDOOR   SENIORS

CHERRY
3933 Brown

Sizes 11 to 9
All the fittings

JANIE
3956 Brown

Sizes 2 to 9
All the fittings

LINDY
3984 Brown

Sizes 11 to 8½
All the fittings

INDOOR   JUNIORS

CHERRY
3933 Brown

Sizes 11 to 9
All the fittings

primary and hope for the best . . . So if you're going to plan
ahead, now, which I think is the only thing you can do in
the circumstances . . . what I suggest is a with-profits
endowment policy linked to a seven-year maturity date with
yearly incrementals – optional, if you like, or you can build
them in, it depends how optimistic you are about your
career, ha ha – leaving a little bit of the schools fees to pay at
the time, but there will be a big chunk taken out, that's for
sure . . . and do it off monthly standing orders of around
. . . let's say . . . five hundred a month?

He looks up hopefully at EMMA and RICHARD. RICHARD's eyes roll up in
his head and he passes out.

10   INT. EMMA & RICHARD'S BEDROOM. NIGHT.

EMMA and RICHARD are in various states of undress as they go to bed.
They are also having a huge fight.

> EMMA   . . . He's my son!
> RICHARD   . . . He's *my* son!

RICHARD disappears into the bathroom. Turns the washbasin taps on.
EMMA yells to him from the bedroom.

> EMMA   I do NOT want him going to some –
> RICHARD   *I* went to a state school –
> (*from the
> bathroom*)
> EMMA   They were different, then –

'New bugs are wets and weeds their mummies blub when they kiss them goodbye while seniors such as me hem-hem stand grimly by licking their slobering chops. No more dolies or William the bear to cuddle and hug, no more fairy stories at nanny's knee it is all aboard the fairy bus for the dungeons. You hav to hav a bit of patience but once the train moves out the little victims are YOURS. You put them in the lugage rack with molesworth 2.

Paters at the moment are patting the blubing maters. 'It is all right old gurl,' they sa. 'Skools are not wot they were in my day. Boys are no longer cruel to each other and the masters are frends.'

'But my Eustace hav been taken away. He is only a baby.'

(*You are dead right he is. Fancy sending him to skool with a name like Eustace. They deserve it all.*)

Pater stare at his glass of gin reflectively. It will be peaceful at home now. He can relax at the weekends and if it is a good skool Eustace will soon be strong and brany enuff to bring in the coal.'

Geoffrey Willans,
How to be Topp

RICHARD emerges from the bathroom. His mouth is full of foaming
toothpaste. He talks a trifle thickly.

> RICHARD   There's absolutely nothing wrong with the place up the road.

DADDY WANTS ME TO WORK HARD SO AS TO GROW UP AND MAKE ENOUGH MONEY TO SEND MY SON TO THIS DUMP.

EMMA   St Bostick's? Nothing wrong with St Bostick's?
RICHARD   We know two people – three people – who've got their kids –
EMMA   Jane says they end up THREE YEARS behind –
RICHARD   JANE! That . . . *boiler* . . .

He staggers back into the bathroom.

EMMA   She's *very nice* – just because she's *large* –

RICHARD bursts out again. He's trying to floss his teeth now.

RICHARD   Look: how are we going to AFFORD an extra five hundred a
           month? How?
EMMA   Cheaper holidays! I don't know! Work harder!
RICHARD   I can't work any harder! I'm gonna DIE if I work any harder!

EMMA glares at him. And slams the bedroom door in his face. And we hear
the baby starting to cry, from his room. EMMA suddenly comes to – opens
the door again –

EMMA   Richard! We haven't put him down for a nursery school – !
RICHARD   *Damn.*
(from the
bathroom)

Fear and loathing in Bideford

DAY **0**: Pack for West Country, dead of night, barely able to see let alone think. Why all our clothes the same when we hit thirties? For work, put on chainstore collar and tie. For leisure, put on chainstore polo-type shirt and slacks. Only difference is in cost. Examine filthy battered weekend trousers and deformed suede shoes. Am I really going to wear these in public? Let's face it, wear them already for Saturday shop in Waitrose along with thousands of other middle-class fathers all dressed as derelicts in the wines section (A nice little Pouilly Fuissé? Pardon me while I tuck the arse back into my trousers). Nod off while musing on homogeneity of clothes. Awoken by four-year-old on way to lavatory. Asks if I'm drunk.

DAY **1**: Forget to put water in car radiator. Red light glows moodily all way down M4. Four-year-old throws up promiscuously over seat, his going-on-holiday trousers, his sister. Too much orange juice at the Leigh Delamere services. Get to Bideford, five in afternoon, feeling like unchanged nappy. Cottage hiding behind dank shrubbery like diorama of prehistoric Europe in Nat. Hist. Museum. Green paint on woodwork could be moss. Woman who owns place has wall-eye and red setter.

DAY **2**: Discover that forgot to pack corkscrew, tea-towels, book of 101 Interesting Walks, storybook about Bear That Can't Play Piano, contraceptives. Countryside steamy; hairy, endless roads. Takes 15 minutes to drive 6 miles into centre of Bideford due to endlessness of roads and imbecilic road signs. Have to *ask* for contraceptives at chemist's, not just wave items pinkly at assistant. So no get contraceptives, but eczema cream instead. Kids fight over supper, get (a) bloody nose (b) poke in the eye and (c) break wall-eyed woman's willow-pattern dish. That's ten quid gone.

DAY **3**: At last. Begin to feel holiday effect taking over. Kids play among stinging-nettles, red setter shit, thistles, horse-flies, wormcasts, slime. Get tight at lunchtime, make indecent suggestion to wife, but no contraceptives and anyway, kids urgent to see sea. See sea. Sea colour of a heavy cold. Plan great excursion (no more than 15 miles, otherwise whole day gone in negotiating anarchic Devon goat-tracks) for next day. Why bring Hunter S. Thompson's *Fear And Loathing in Las Vegas* along to read? Why? Monstrous symbolism of travel book which makes world seem like Vision of Hell while enjoying miniature Vision of Hell in West Country. Still, better than Patrick Leigh Fermor, endless garbage about local customs, ravishing scenery, enchanting cranky locals.

DAYS **4, 5, 6, 7**:

No sun-tan cream! Unbelievable! Bideford, July, it's hot enough to give you sunburn! Kids go pleasant egg brown. Wife turns colour of strawberry Instant Whip. I go colour of rump steak, feel like burning cigarette end all over shoulders, thighs, feet. Skin generally starting to age like old handbag or bodywork of car: not bad at distance, but close to, mysteriously patterned, like surface of Mars. Consign shorts to drawer, too dangerous in this heat. Unable to do anything in bed but lie and whimper so temporarily give up search for progressive chemist who keeps contraceptives out on display. Kids break ancient irreplaceable pale green conical Woolworth's cup belonging to Mrs Wall-Eye. That's another tenner. Get plastered in evening, discover that stars in countryside amazing, mystical light show, full of majesty of Heaven, great glowing firmament, feel like student all over again, wide-eyed at wonderfulness of things, trip and fall into primitive ha-ha at end of garden. Sunburn agony as wife (also drunk and gigglingly unsympathetic with it) pulls me out. Kids getting restless. Make for funfair tomorrow.

DAY **8**: Would it have been better with another family on board? Whole week of holiday now gone, but still working 23 hours out of 24 minding potties, cooking food, searching for lost particle of Lego, shopping for sweets and icecreams and exploding drinks, explaining in most genteel terms available why horse in nearby field has permanent erection. With other family, could we have left kids with *them* and gone off to taste vibrant sophisticated Bideford nightlife (Lobster Pot restaurant, fully licensed, folk singing Thursdays)? Take funfair, for instance. Reptile in charge of Magic Roundabout clearly loathes children after twenty years of roundabout rides, encourages smallest most ill-coordinated kids to perch on top of vast heaving wood and plaster horse in hope that when ride begins movement will hurl child into machinery for ever. So have to scamper round perimeter of operating roundabout shouting instructions to two-year-old while preventing four-year-old (riding Prancer) from taking out small Birmingham person on Tosca next to him with his fists. Wife is launched on True Love (gelding) next to two-year-old but unable to help since vertigo attack follows first movement of horse's pole. Result: carnage averted but father left in state of deep physical and nervous distress. Could it have been avoided with extra couple plus extra kids?

DAY **9**: Tormented by notion that should have spent holiday with Jack and Kate from next door but seven.

DAY **10**: Wife reminds me (in middle of torment about Jack and Kate) that actually *had* holiday with Jack and Kate and their three children in rented midden near Colwyn Bay. Points out that even though no more than week long, seemed to last approx. 2000 years given their children with talent for running away from home/eating razor blades/climbing into boot of car to die/vomiting continuously/fighting with our children in between asthma bouts. Also I had drunken row with Jack, day two, for which neither party could bring himself to apologize and which polluted friendship forever. Also that Kate had mild breakdown and shut self in bathroom for day and a half. Also that I described them in car on way home as five most grotesque examples of humanity this side of the swamps of Lousiana. Amazing how I seem to have forgotten all this. Why is it women can remember absolutely everything, all the time?

DAY **11**: Suddenly realize, might be in *wrong cottage*. Haul out section from *Times* brought along in case of dispute:

THE REAL MOROCCO – Three weeks from £450. Marrakesh, Casablanca, Fez, Tangier. Expert guides, authentic cuisine, genuine accommodation, insurance included. ABTA member. Leatherhead 29786.

TUSCANY – Fourteenth-century palazzo, sleeps twenty-three, own vineyard, olive grove, swimming pool, tennis court, frescoes by Masaccio, forty-five minutes from Florence, stunning location, £15 p.w. Leatherhead 29786.

DUNGENESS – Family holidays. Caravan, sleeps four. Leatherhead 29786.

CHEAP FLIGHTS – Athens, Tunis, Tangier, Rome, Leningrad, Novosibirsk. Save on family bookings. CCCP Airways. Leatherhead 29786.

BIDEFORD – Delightful three-bed cottage, views over Bideford Bay, own washing-machine, children welcome, still some vacancies for July/August, ring Leatherhead 29786.

Frantic thoughts overwhelm me. Where view over Bay as promised? Where washing-machine as promised? Where delightful? But then, where other punters, hammering to get in? How come Mrs Wall-Eye know my name? So *where view of Bay?*

DAY **12**: Nearly total car on roundabout near Muddiford again. Wife maintains that my driving is getting worse. I argue that rear axle radius location arm must be out of true. Realize I have no idea what I'm talking about, but refuse to back down. Visit insanely disorganised Living Steam Museum, with exploding traction engines running over kids, madmen in filthy overalls charging in uncontrollable diagonals across field, fires breaking out everywhere, doom-laden barn exhibition of hideous implements. Daughter bursts into screaming fit when jovial psycopath sounds steam whistle on boiling traction engine two feet from where we are standing. Nearly crash car again, as I pass what looks from the road like a progressive-minded chemist, but which turns out to be a printer's shop.

DAY **13**: Realise that we should never have gone on holiday with *Jack and Kate*, but with *Harry and Chrissie* and their child. Put this to the wife who strikes me a blow with the potato-masher.

What *did* we see, last holidays?

- An exhibition of domestic utensils and farm implements
- A two foot gauge steam railway
- A collection of traditional and contemporary lead glass
- A pencil museum
- A flamingo park
- A watermill
- A children's theme park with 'Crazy Critters' show, Animated Nursery Rhymes and Toddlers Town
- A cheese dairy
- A coal mining museum with a difference

Until you come you cannot know how delightful it is at **Butlin's**

So many acres of lovely, quiet gardens . . . such pleasantly appointed sun lounges . . . such service everywhere . . . such smiling champagne air . . . such wonderful sands and countryside . . . so much beautiful and interesting complete change from the everyday world . . . such a nice people to meet . . . truly a *real* holiday that will always remain a happy memory.

Will you be my guest,
and see for yourself? *W. E. Butlin*

AYR (Scotland)
PWLLHELI (Wales)   CLACTON (Essex)
SKEGNESS (Lincolnshire)   FILEY (East Yorkshire)
MOSNEY (Ireland)

We think you may be interested in further details and illustrated brochure, which may be obtained free from —
BUTLIN'S LTD. Dept. H.B. 439 OXFORD ST., LONDON W.1
— or your local Agents.

DAY **13**: Penultimate day. Wife determined to do something BIG. Picnic on headland, stately home, walk over hills, followed by Great Family Supper which I have to cook. But I am too busy looking for View of Bay as specified in advertisement. Only one part of cottage pointing in right direction, i.e. rear part, but even from kids' bedroom only trees visible. Until try small shabby door on landing: which opens up on to flight of filthy stairs going up into cobwebbed, dust-laden attic smelling of undiscovered murders, with tiny dormer window, size of large paperback. Through pre-war grime . . . can just make out sea. *So where washing-machine?*

DAY **14**: Most extraordinary thing: as wife shoves high-chair into car's rear suspension and I quietly herniate myself on a couple of bags filled with Devon mud and light aggregate thieved from local quarry by children, strange sense of loss creeps over me. The holiday is over. Children play mournfully in heap of setter shit above which washing-line used to hang (until sodden towel bust it at three a.m., landing in setter ordure as mentioned). Feeling of nostalgia is in the air like mist. Ghastly dwarf's cottage now looks quaint, appealing, homely. Impossible lanes now merely playful. May have to return next year, depending on finances.

DAY **15**: At last get around to unpacking bags, back at home. Unwrap unused bathing suit. *Find contraceptives.*

THE WHOLE POINT OF THE COUNTRY IS TO RECONCILE YOU TO LONDON.

Sixtysomething

SCENE ONE

Scene: the drawing-room of a house somewhere in the country. Chintz armchairs and well-worn rugs set the tone. A large old-fashioned sideboard holds the drinks. A pair of french windows opens out on to a view of a well-tended garden. It is spring. The sun shines in.

DAVID:	(*off*) NO! I don't *want* it on my trousers.
	(*pause*)
JANET:	(*off*) It won't clean off, David.
DAVID:	(*off*) Damn.
NED:	(*off*) *Dad.* I've killed you. Lie down.
	(GRAMPS *enters.*)
GRAMPS:	(*shouting through the windows*) Stop mucking about on my bulbs. Little bugger.
DAVID:	(*off*) Sorry.
	(GRAMPS *pours himself a drink. Sits down*)
GRAMPS:	Well? Doesn't anyone want to come and talk to me?
	(*blackout*)

SCENE TWO

Scene: the dining-room. As the drawing-room, but no armchairs. Instead a large, old-fashioned dining table. GRAMPS, GRAN, JANET, DAVID, NED *and* OLLY *(the baby) are seated round it, having Sunday lunch.*

GRAMPS:	(*in the middle of a spiel*) So we thought, first the Caribbean for a couple of weeks, then, later in the year, your mother quite wants to see the Great Wall of China before she's too old. Who was it who went to China? Was it the Walkers?
GRAN:	It was the Woods.
GRAMPS:	The Woods. They went to China. Loved China.
GRAN:	*She* didn't.
GRAMPS:	No, she didn't.

> The number of people in England and Wales over the age of 75
> has increased by 20 per cent since 1981; and those over 85 by
> almost 40 per cent, according to the Office of Population
> Censuses and Surveys.

GRAN: Are you all right for gravy, dear? Would you like some more meat?

DAVID: (*stifled by the unwonted amount of food he's eating*) Er . . . that's fine, thanks, Mum. Delicious.

GRAN: Janet? More meat? More potato? Swede? Peas? Yorkshire pudding? Gravy? Horseradish? It's home-made.

JANET: I couldn't, thanks –

NED: I want some more.

GRAN: Well, maybe Grandpa will help you to some more –

GRAMPS: Are you sure it was the Woods?

GRAN: It was.

GRAMPS: Oh.
(*– beat. As an afterthought –*)
How's the work, going, David?

DAVID: Er –
(*blackout*)

SCENE THREE

Scene: the garden. DAVID *and* JANET *are having a muttered conversation as they examine the bulbs.*

JANET: Can't you ask him?

DAVID: Outright?

JANET: Why not?

DAVID: 'Listen, Dad. I'm skint. You've saved a bit. What about the school fees, then?' Something like that?

> According to a MORI poll (*How and Why Parents Choose
> an Independent School*) around seven per cent of all parents
> with children at an independent school enjoy the benefits of
> a trust fund, set up by a relative.

108

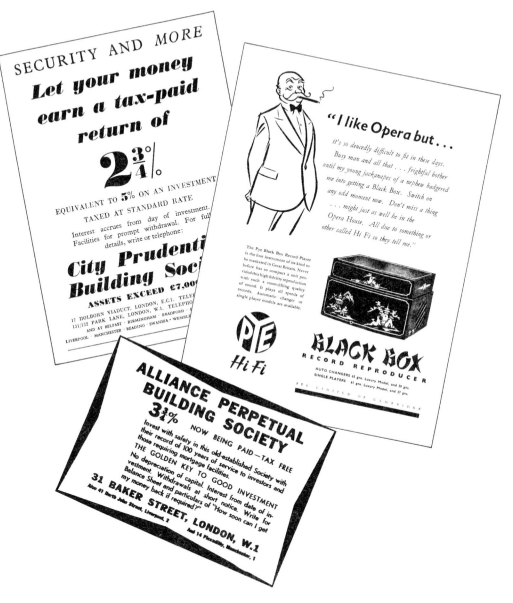

JANET: Ever thought of *tact*?

DAVID: I can't stand crawling.

JANET: Either he's patronizing you or you're patronizing him. Or both.

NED: (*running on*) Dad! Grandpa's got a lawnmower with a seat! (*blackout*)

SCENE FOUR

The drawing-room. GRAMPS *is seated comfortably in an armchair.* DAVID *is staring tensely out of the window.*

GRAMPS: No question, old boy, you won't go short when I die. You and your sister. This house has to be worth three hundred. I've got a bit saved. Then there's your mother's bits and pieces when she goes. It all adds up.
(*beat*)
'Course, we might live to be ninety. Then we'd have spent it all. Ha!

. . . And then in the middle of the funeral wake
With her mouth full of excellent Madeira cake
His widow cried, 'That's done,
My life's at last begun,
Sing Hallelujah, Hey nonny-no,
Hey nonny-no, Hey nonny-no,
It's time I had some fun,
Today though hardly a jolly day,
At least has set me free,
We'll all have a lovely holiday
On the island of Capri!

In a bar on the Piccola Marina
Life called to Mrs Wentworth-Brewster . . .

Noel Coward, *A Bar On The Piccola Marina*

(*beat*)

GRAMPS: Actually, I've got a bit of cash, some policy I'd forgotten about just realized, I was wondering what to do with it. You'd probably know. Do you think I should put it on deposit at the Nat West; or put it into Savings Certificates; or Unit Trusts; or just spend it?

DAVID: (*strangled*) I . . .

GRAMPS: Your mother was saying perhaps I should give it to the kids, half to you, half to Debbie, but I said, no. Said you wouldn't like it. What do you think?

DAVID: I wouldn't mind if . . .

GRAMPS: You think Unit Trusts?

DAVID: (*more strangled*) Savings Certificates –

GRAMPS: So *safe*. You're so *safe*. No spark. Never had any spark. Unlike that girl you married. She's got spark. Enough for two. I bet she keeps you up to the mark.

(*Pause.* GRAMPS *contemplates his fingernails. Continues –*)

Then again, I wondered if I shouldn't leave it to charity. The Home For Distressed Rabbits is a favourite of mine at the moment.

(DAVID *emits a small cry*)

Have you made a will, old boy?

'25th. (Christmas-day.) My wife began, I know not whether by design or chance, to enquire what she should do, if I should by any accident die, to which I did give her some slight answer, but shall make good use of it to bring myself to some settlement for her sake, by making a will as soon as I can.'

Samuel Pepys, *Diary*

DAVID: I'm only thirty-seven.

GRAMPS: Shouldn't leave it. Get run down by a tram to-morrow –

DAVID: They don't have trams any more.

GRAMPS: Figuratively. I'm entitled to my exaggeration. An old man's whim. You've got dependants.

DAVID: Yes, but I haven't got anything to leave them.

GRAMPS: Haven't you? I think at your time of life you should.

DAVID: I –

(*blackout*)

111

SCENE FIVE

Scene: the kitchen. GRAN *is there, setting a tray with tea things.* JANET *watches, knowing she will not be allowed to help.* OLLY *is at floor level. The kitchen is almost abnormally clean and tidy.*

GRAN: . . . So I said, why on earth don't you take it round the front, you see? But he either couldn't or wouldn't understand, and he left it at the back. Why do they bother? Why do they set themselves up as tradesmen if that's all they're going to do? Before the war, as my mother would have told you, a workman always knocked twice at the back door before even taking his hat off. Do *you* have a daily? Or do you do everything yourself? We have a Mrs Doings, and the place is still untidy. Of course, your house is so lovely and full of life. Have you ever thought of giving up work and being a full-time mother? It must be such a difficult decision to make, what with the little one, and Ben just about to start school . . .
(OLLY *lets out a window-bursting scream*)
Poor baby . . .
(JANET *picks him up*)

JANET: He'll be fine, no problem, just wanted to cry . . .

GRAN: Would you like me to hold him? Does he need burping? A fresh nappy? Do you want to take him outside? Would he like some milk? I can wash his bottle out in two minutes. Are you sure he doesn't need burping? The poor little mite. Aren't they treating you properly, then? Are you saying, I want some attention, I don't get enough of it because Mummy's always too busy? Does he want some baby food? I've got a jar here somewhere . . .

JANET: He'll be *fine* . . .

GRAN: What was I saying? Oh, David's father, he's such an old stick nowadays, he wants everyone to jump to attention when he comes in the room. And now he's pestering poor David to make a will. David's already made a will, hasn't he? What with the children and the school fees. I wish there was some way we could help. But of course there isn't.
(*blackout*)

SCENE SIX

The Garden again. GRAMPS *is gallantly propelling* JANET *around the flowerbeds.*

GRAMPS: Just between you and me, I had a visit the other day, from a very interesting young man.

JANET: Oh yes?

GRAMPS: Fascinating young man. Property

JANET: Property?

GRAMPS: Abroad. Brilliant notion. They build a villa in Spain, somewhere hot and sunny. They create twenty-six different leaseholds. Each leasehold runs for two weeks of each year, at a particular time. They then sell these leaseholds to chaps like me. And chaps like me can then go down to the villa, for those two weeks, every year for the next twenty-five years, without paying a penny! We effectively own the property! Brilliant, eh?

JANET: A timeshare?

GRAMPS: Ah, no. Not a timeshare. A . . . a sharetime, I think it was.

JANET: You didn't give this man any money, did you?

GRAMPS: Only the deposit, so far.

JANET: How much was that?

GRAMPS: Oh, you wouldn't be interested. Not the sort of thing you want to worry about.

JANET: A thousand? Two thousand? Three?

GRAMPS: Ten thousand, actually. I think I've done rather well, there. Course the balance is due next week. Then I get a look at the title deeds. Address in Leatherhead, I think it came from.

JANET: *(her jaw sagging)* Oh my God . . .

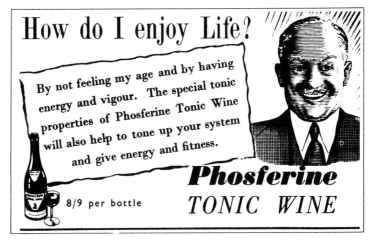

SCENE SEVEN

Scene: in the car.

JANET: Nothing we can do?
DAVID: Nothing.
JANET: Is the old boy bats, or what?
DAVID: He's my father –
JANET: Sorry.
             (*beat*)
NED: Dad!
DAVID: Yes?
NED: Don't you ever stop talking about money?
             (*blackout*)

How do people spend the money left to them in a legacy?

49% save it
21% buy property
15% let it go on general consumption
6% spend it on home improvements
4% spend it on holidays
4% buy a car with it
1% use it to pay school fees

Source: Housing Research Foundation

In 1989, the dead bequeathed £14.7 billion to the living.

A DECENT STORY.

What we believe

DIALOGUE THE SECOND: COOLING OUT

'They were so different from the people we knew in London that it was quite difficult. Their topics of conversation seemed very limited compared to what we talked about at home. They didn't seem to be very bothered about issues other than what was going on in the village itself. In fact, they later changed my philosophy of life. I feel now that if everybody looked after their own surroundings or took more notice of what's going on immediately around them, the world might be a better place . . .'

Woman who moved from London to a Suffolk village, talking about the inhabitants.

It is the fourth day of the month of June, and HARRY and PHIL are walking together in the garden of HARRY's house. It is on the subject of change and changing circumstances that they speak.

HARRY: If it is true that no man knows what may befall him, nor how he may make himself safe against all future evils, is it not therefore the wisest course to make no provision, but to live in the present experience only?

PHIL: That is the Fallacy of *Carpe Diem*.

HARRY: How might you explain that?

PHIL: The Fallacy of *Carpe Diem* is a falsely reasoned argument which concludes that it is best to enjoy the momentary pleasure, and have no thought for the consequences it may bring. That it is wrong, we may learn from the sights all around us: drunken men lying on the ground, cursing and making oaths; young women lost to the bondage of early motherhood, always

115

HE IS WISE IN THE WAYS OF PENSIONS AND PERSONAL INVESTMENT.

pushing children about in small carts, and making oaths;
reckless gamblers who by their own improvidence must sell
double-glazing for the prudent man's windows. Their god is
Carpe Diem – 'Seize the present day'. By seizing the present, they
have let Nemesis seize them.

HARRY: What, then, ought they to have done?

PHIL: In truth, a man is bound to take care of the present, and by so
doing, take care of the future also. He must seek the advice of
the wisest money-brokers and buy a pension scheme if he be
self-employed; he must see to it that he does not over-extend
himself on the mortgage front; he must run a motor car that
doesn't drink petrol like tapwater and won't break him every
time it needs a service from a franchised dealer; above all, he
must abstain from vicious pleasures – or if he needs must
indulge, then he must do so only in moderation. This is the
argument of Epicurus the Greek, whose teachings have since
been much corrupted.

HARRY: That is to say, he must take care, and not go off the rails.

PHIL: Indeed.

HARRY: Then what have you to say to my argument, which is that by not going off the rails, man is destined to live meanly and dully, and in that way corrupts the true purpose of his being on earth?

PHIL: Come again?

HARRY: That, if you spend the span of your life making sure that you'll still be here in twenty-five years' time, you're wasting your life away. Who cares if you don't save? Something always comes up. You've got to *live*. Otherwise what's the point of being alive?

PHIL: But that is, as I have said, the Fallacy of *Carpe Diem*.

HARRY: But it is my philosophy. And as you see, I am still here, still alive, still able to enjoy all the pleasures that mind and body may afford.

PHIL: Yes, but look at you.

HARRY: What's that supposed to mean?

PHIL: You look like a bum.

HARRY: What do you mean, I look like a bum?

> 'Jan van Hogspeuw staggers to the door
> And pisses at the dark. Outside, the rain
> Courses in cart-ruts down the deep mud lane.
> Inside, Dirk Dogstoerd pours himself some more,
> And holds a cinder to his clay with tongs,
> Belching out smoke. Old Prijck snores with the gale,
> His skull face firelit; someone behind drinks ale,
> And opens mussels, and croaks scraps of songs
> Towards the ham-hung rafters about love.
> Dirk deals the cards. Wet century-wide trees
> Clash in surrounding starlessness above
> This lamplit cave, where Jan turns back and farts,
> Gobs at the grate, and hits the queen of hearts.
>
> Rain, wind and fire! The secret, bestial peace!'
>
> Philip Larkin, *The Card-Players*

PHIL: There are holes in your pullover, your Barbour is in the last stage of decrepitude and your trousers can't have been near a press in months.

HARRY: I live in the country. This is how people look in the country.

PHIL: But five years ago you had a good job, prospects, a nice house, money in the bank. You were clean and tidy.

HARRY: That is true. But it is commonly held that Mind and Matter both have existence, separately, one from the other. Plato, Descartes, Spinoza and Bergson have all descanted on the subject. My belief is that whatever material circumstance we enjoy, the promptings of the mind have a life unto themselves. The promptings of my mind told me to get out of computing and go to live in Shropshire on a small dairy farm making highly profitable specialist products such as goat's milk yoghurt, sheep's cheese and traditional butter. As it might be, the little kingdom which is Harry Kirkpatrick was subject to an insurrection, or rebellion. It was a rebellion which led me to take wife and kids from the suburbs into the peace of the countryside. As a consequence, I do look a bit on the ragged side. But that's Shropshire, you see. It's very beautiful where I live, and the kids love it.

PHIL: And this has made you happy?

HARRY: What is happiness?

PHIL: It is the state of pleasurable content of mind, which results from success or the attainment of what is considered good.

HARRY: Then I am happy, in that I have attained what *you* would call success; and happy, in that I have attained what *I* consider good.

PHIL: But your circumstances are precarious, and may easily lead you into unhappiness. That is my point: you have cast aside the probability of future happiness on a whim.

HARRY: You sound like my old Dad.

PHIL: I do?

HARRY: I am thirty-eight years old, but the way he went on about my profligacy, short-sightedness and general pansying about made me feel twelve all over again.

PHIL: Well, I think the old boy had a point.

Rural life's not what it used to be

Property

● Getting away from it all. CAROLINE McGHIE weighs up the headaches and rising cost of a second home in the country – and wonders if perhaps a weekend hotel break would do instead

DECIDING between buying a country cottage or taking well-timed country weekend breaks in a little hotel is one of life's eternal highly-charged conundrums. In the present market the whole issue becomes fudged with talk of capital gains and investment, as if thatch and green fields were suddenly some new kind of commodity or share issue.

As higher prices ripple out off the commuter track, the weekend cottage has become an expensive luxury, the kind of bacon, and all...

centives will be less obvious. Letting a second home is not known for being financially rewarding. Experts estimate about a 3½ per cent return on the capital value before estimate as maintenance expenses such And the old gardener down the lane who might in years have brought in years the grass and while

...much for sale at £... away from other people at ... weekends.... And there's ... when you get ... night and ...

Dream for sale: Cherrytrees in Stoke-by...

Property

Once upon a time lost in a forest glade...

DRIVE through the beech trees down an unmarked track on the edge of the Stourhead pleasure gardens in Wiltshire and press through more than a mile-long tunnel of firs, bracken and foxgloves. At the end there is the kind of cottage Hansel and Gretel could have stumbled upon.

● CAROLINE McGHIE discovers a fairy-tale cottage and finds that similar properties are selling very fast

The Convent in the Woods, an eighteenth century gothic folly set in a clearing of wild daisies and rare trees, would have been an uncommon proposition a few years ago. The rights to spend a third of the year there can be bought for £55,000 or more. (The price for this curious arrangement is understandably difficult to set.)

Such is the scramble this summer for period cottages that it will sell very quickly. Any property that is old and looks like a picture postcard, is likely these days to have five would-be buyers pitching for it.

The Convent in the Woods has special qualities. It offers an end to solution to the shortage of period properties (split them all into three what we wanted), with its sophisticated timeshare system which is perfect for busy people who like to go away for weekends. Each of the three partners gets a week or weekend in strict rotation, though weekends can be swapped and special arrangements can be made for school holidays.

It demands that the partners share a view of life. The little house with crusted stone walls, turrets and gothic windows, is lit by candles which shed an intriguing smoke stain over the ceilings. There are flagstones, lamps, huge log baskets, well-worn padded linen curtains to keep out the winter cold, stained glass windows and endless other ecclesiastical architectural references.

The water pours from taps only because it is pumped up to a large tank on the hill behind by a waterwheel. It is spring water and deliciously sweet. Almost everything is kept in period with the house because that is the way the owners, two architects and an owner of an art gallery, wanted it. Now that one is opting out, a new partner must be found.

They bought the three-bedroom

Picture-postcard stuff: a new partner is needed to help run the Convent in the Woods, an eighteenth century gothic folly in Wiltshire

convent in a state of near-collapse five years ago from the National Trust with the promise they would restore it faithfully, which has been done with extraordinary flair. The huge sitting room with doors on to the garden and an eccentric ceiling with thousands of stones set in horsehair plaster, has been pictured in numerous magazines. There are still ambitious plans to be realised, especially in the gardens.

Archie Hunter, of the Knight Frank & Rutley office in Sherborne, Dorset, which is marketing the house, said: "More and more people are chasing fewer and fewer period properties. We can spend many days showing people round them. One house we wild recently – well outside the magic two-hour journey from London – had 200 people interested in it and over 50 actually went round it."

In Marlborough, Wiltshire, Iain Cowan of Dreweatt Neate has resorted to selling houses by the "best offers" system to avoid gazumping. "Period houses here invariably sell for around 10% more than the asking price because there is an over-demand and under-supply. Prices have probably increased in the last three months by 20% so it is hard for us to keep pace." he said.

"I like to give people a guide price and then ask them to make sealed bids, which I open on a specific day and accept the highest," he explained. He currently has 800 buyers searching for homes between £50,000 and £250,000 and 50% of those are looking above £250,000 with cash.

With the latest figures from the Royal Institution of Chartered Surveyors (Rics) showing that accelerating house prices, once the preserve of London and the south-east, are spreading to all areas at a rate of between 2% and over 8% in the last three months alone, it is hardly surprising that the competition is so fierce.

For first-time buyers it can be very said. Jane Tant, director of First Time Home Buyers' Advisory Service, blames the overheating of the market on the abrupt limitation of tax relief to £30,000 per home by August 1. "My fears have been realised. Nineteen of our help in obtaining a mortgage were gazumped. This is much the highest proportion ever recorded." she said.

Talk of gazumping always makes estate agents jittery because they are often pilloried for operating a system which allows it to happen. But as a Rics spokesman said: "The estate agent is under contract to report all offers to his client, the seller. It is then up to the client whether he wants to gazump or not.

HARRY: And are you happy with your pointlessly expensive urban house with its coffee-and-cream décor and its bristling gadgets, your sixty-five-minute slog into work every day, your overheated office with the 'phone shrilling in your ear, your tiresomely predictable holidays, your interests in food, jogging and American films of the 1940s, your car which is always getting scratched, and your kids and the mortgage and the bills and all that? That makes you happy?

PHIL: My point is, that it is better to be prudent than happy.

HARRY: But you brought it up.

PHIL: I did?

HARRY: You asked if I was happy.

PHIL: Well, then, let me put it this way: neither you nor I is happy; but I may at least continue to be only moderately unhappy in reasonable comfort, while you may abruptly cease to be anything at all except on Social Security if goat's cheese and sheep's yoghurt hit a rough patch. Which is the greater evil?

HARRY: You're bats.

PHIL: I think it's a cop-out. It'll end in tears.

HARRY: But it wouldn't be worth doing, if there wasn't a chance that it might end in tears. That's axiomatic.

PHIL: Then I ask: how would you feel if everyone else cooled out like you?

HARRY: But not everyone else could cool out. You cannot cool out if everyone cools with you. That is also axiomatic.

PHIL: So your position is dependent on the rest of us remaining cooled in?

HARRY: To some degree, that is true.

PHIL: Would it therefore be reasonable to say that you enjoy your way of life by the dispensation of people like me?

HARRY: Don't you try and get clever.